Over the past decade, **Owen Eastwood** has worked with some of the most elite teams and groups in the world, including Gareth Southgate's England Football team, the British Olympic team, NATO and the South African Cricket Team – coaching their leaders on how to build world-class cultures and take performance to the highest level.

'A copy of Eastwood's new book, *Belonging*, was given to every England player when they reported for duty at the European Championships'   – *Daily Telegraph*

'*Belonging* is a must-read for anyone interested in building a long term high-performing team'   – Stuart Lancaster

'One of the wisest books about winning you'll ever read . . . Powerful lessons beautifully expressed'   – James Kerr

'Owen's work and outlook really resonate with me. His philosophy has real depth and value. [It's] so of the moment – at just the right time, at just the right place, with just the right message'   – Simon Mundie

Belonging

Unlock Your Potential with the Ancient Code of Togetherness

Owen Eastwood

QUERCUS

First published in Great Britain in 2021 by Quercus.
This paperback edition published in 2022 by

QUERCUS

Quercus Editions Ltd
Carmelite House
50 Victoria Embankment
London EC4Y 0DZ

An Hachette UK company

A CIP catalogue record for this book is available
from the British Library

PB (B) ISBN 978 1 52941 031 0
PB (A) ISBN 978 1 52942 383 9
Ebook ISBN 978 1 52941 032 7

10 9 8 7 6 5 4

Typeset by CC Book Production Ltd
Printed and bound in Great Britain by Clays Ltd, Elcograf S.p.A.

Papers used by Quercus Editions Ltd are from well-managed forests and other responsible sources.

To Elizabeth, Tom & Livvy
and every soul who has gifted to another a sense of belonging

Contents

Prologue

Prologue

Over the years, I've taken some leaders I've coached to a beautiful valley near where I live in the Cotswolds area of England. It is a place called Snowshill.

We stand on a rise and look out over this magnificent valley.

In a crease at the bottom of a gully runs a stream, lined with beech trees. On top of the hill on the other side of the valley lies a dense ancient woodland, flooded with bluebells. Between us and the stream sheep, cattle and horses graze on the slopes.

There is a well-worn path in the grass, imprinted by thousands of footsteps. From where we stand on that hill, this path meanders down the gully, to the stream, and then rises steeply up the other side, to the watchful ancient woodland.

Together, we look into the valley.

We reflect that for over 99 per cent of human history our ancestors lived in bands of hunter-gatherers in valleys like this one.

We consider how, as a species, we transformed ourselves from foragers to predators. How this involved confronting the vulnerability of living in open grasslands: wild animals, uncontrollable climate, inconsistent food supply and competition from other humans.

On Snowshill, we see clearly that the crucial adaptation we made as a species was to form strongly bonded groups. We understood from the start that survival as individuals would be hopeless.

This ability to form strong organised groups became the true 'super strength' of *homo sapiens* – our competitive advantage.

We think about how the strongest, most trustworthy group we could belong to was kin. From kin, we formed communities and tribes. Their essential purpose the same – to protect and compete. People needed to be taken care of. A village needed feeding. A way of life to sustain. Within our tribes we built teams to enable all of this.

We contemplate how this shift to group living changed our biology and our psychological needs.

We look into the valley and our imagination paints a picture of ancestral teams working together, men and women: hunting, gathering, herding, building, exploring, caring. Each person with a role to play and a task to perform.

We can see how a common way of working emerged in these teams. How standards materialised of what was and what was not acceptable in the shared interests of the group. How we converted experience into teaching. How we rejected a fixed understanding of what was possible.

Communal connections grew stronger but were never taken for granted or assumed. Around the fire our language revealed itself, giving life to stories of the known and unknown worlds.

We diverged from the hierarchical ways of other primates. We became more egalitarian. Expectations of being treated fairly

4

emerged. The benefit of the group overrode everything else. On this, our ancestors were clear – the alphas hunted with the pack.

On Snowshill, time dissolves before our eyes, like the mist that surrounds us, the same mist our ancestors walked through.

On a biting autumn afternoon in 2019, in a room within the cloisters of Magdalen College, Oxford University, I met with Professor Robin Dunbar, one of the world's leading evolutionary psychologists.

Early in our meeting a powerful insight surfaced, to the surprise of both of us. Robin asked me to take him into the 'dressing room', so to speak, of a high-performing team today and describe how they might be organised and led. After I did this, Robin replied, 'That is in essence the same way hunter-gatherers set themselves up sixty thousand years ago.'

Robin took me back into *homo sapien*'s evolutionary story and together we mapped primal human needs that still direct us today: our need to belong converted into an emotive identity story; our need for a shared purpose transformed into a vision of the future; our need for shared beliefs to be translated into a code of how to behave.

Another realisation dawned on me as I travelled home that day. Perhaps, without the distraction of our systems and technology and data, our ancestors understood better than us what makes some teams strong and others weak. After all, they only had each other to rely on. Maybe our ancestors had attempted to convey this knowledge to us but perhaps we'd stopped listening. We'd developed a conceit that we knew better than those before us.

As a result, maybe this super strength of our species is weakening before our eyes. Leaders having forgotten that their first role is to protect their people and that strong groups of *homo sapiens* form when we focus on what we share rather than what divides us.

Over most of our history as a species such mistakes would have been catastrophic. Without our super-strength ability to form strong groups we would have been destined to extinction well before now.

I began to see that wrapped in the stories and spiritual ideas passed down to us were practical lessons drawn from thousands of years of experience. These stories and ideas disclose how to build strong teams and are weighted with emotion to make them durable.

In my work as a performance coach, I've always invoked ancient stories and spiritual beliefs. I was not formally taught these but discovered them through life as I explored the wilds of my own identity. The way I articulate and use these ideas is personal and often unconventional.

I noticed that everywhere I worked and spoke people seemed to connect to ideas from my own culture. This initially surprised me, until I learned that they had their own version of these stories. They were already theirs. That ancient wisdom acquired and passed down is an intrinsic part of our shared human story.

As our communities and teams become increasingly diverse this wisdom has never been more precious.

In the pages that follow, I identify the aspects of teaming that gave *homo sapiens* a competitive advantage. We'll see how these critical elements evolved over time into needs hardwired into our biology and our psychology and how they remain central to who we are today.

We will then see how our ancestors, from all over our world, converted these insights into wisdom.

Finally, we will take a glimpse into the dressing rooms of high-performing teams today to see how these insights continue to underpin great leadership and successful groups of *homo sapiens*.

I have written this book as a tradesman, not as a philosopher. In the work I do, I always come back to the same question: *What is the optimal environment for this group to perform to their best?*

Over time, I've become uncomfortable with the idea that such a small number of people are exposed to these profound insights and our collective ancient wisdom. That does not feel right. All of us can perform at a high level and we should be empowered with the tools to give us that opportunity. In turn, we can unlock how to get the best out of the groups we belong to, from families through to nations. Beyond performance, the environments we operate in have a profound impact on our emotional wellbeing. This has been glossed over for too long.

So, my friend, as the sun breaks through the clouds above Snowshill, let's walk together into this timeless valley.

> *Wisdom is universal and is not confined by generations, by oceans or by cultures. It is part of the legacy of humankind.*
>
> Sir Hirini Moko Mead[1]

1

you belong here

We may not look like it, but we just belong together.

Dr Doolittle

1.1 streams into a river

I come from the south-west corner of the Pacific Ocean.

It is a place where the three most powerful words that can be uttered to you are 'you belong here'.

Over the span of eight hundred years my lines of ancestors, unknown to each other, voyaged across great seas to make their home on the islands where I was born.

Only one line of ancestors already lived within this ocean. The others lived on coastlines of another great ocean. They were pulled away from kin and ways they understood in search of a better life. All of them migrants who became people of this land.

The great chief and navigator Kupe was the first to discover the country where I was born. His crew, led to this new land by a vision, voyaged south-west across 1,700 miles of ocean from our spiritual homeland Hawaiki. With unfathomable skill, they then sailed back to that tiny dot of land in the central Pacific Ocean to share their discovery.

There followed a great fleet of migrating double-hulled vessels to settle these newly discovered islands. One of those sacred canoes, the *Takitimu*, carried my direct ancestor Tahu (after which my Māori tribe *Ngāi Tahu* is named). They landed on the northern island and Tahu became the leader of these people. He voyaged down to the southern island in search of prized greenstone. On this journey he would name a mountain range the Takitimus, after our sacred canoe.

Hundreds of years later my mother, of Irish descent on both sides, her father a Daly, her mother a Casey, was born on a farm at the foot of those same Takitimu Mountains.

My first Irish ancestor to make a home in these islands, Patrick Daly, had exiled himself in the years following the Great Irish Famine in the 1840s. Half of his village, Caherpierce, perished in the famine. Located on the Gaelic-speaking Dingle Peninsula in County Kerry, it was one of the most isolated and poorest parts of Ireland. Fleeing the spectre of starvation and typhus, motivated by fear and hope, my ancestor voyaged across two oceans in search of renewal. That hope justified the price of leaving forever the kin he was born into.

One of Patrick's brothers joined the exodus to North America.

A younger brother stayed at home, only to drown in a nearby river.

One hundred and sixty years later my mother and I visited this ancestral home on the Dingle Peninsula. It was the first time these lines of kin had seen and touched each other since the Great Famine. We ate at their table. We stitched together the past. My mother and I felt a deep sense of belonging to this place despite having never been there before. Prior to leaving, we visited the local church and walked around the gravestones. Staring back at us were the very same names inscribed into our own stones on the other side of the world.

Fate invited another ancestor from another land to our remote islands. One hundred years ago, my English ancestor, my grandfather, voyaged across three oceans to these islands. He had served in the Royal Navy in the First World War. After that war, the Royal Navy sent battle cruisers around the world to pay thanks to the 'colonies' who had shed their own blood for the cause. When this vessel made port at our coastal towns the local community put on dances for the visiting servicemen. At one such dance, my English grandfather would meet a descendant of Tahu, my grandmother Rose. They fell in love and my grandfather was granted a release from the Royal Navy to make his way in this new country. The Government gifted him land on the North Island, in the 'Bay of Plenty', on which to farm. There my father would be born, between a great economic depression and another great war.

All of these people, my ancestors, have their own origin story. They came with their own beliefs and sense of identity forged by the tribes they belonged to. But the world changed around them. They had to move, driven by a vision of something better.

In making a decision to come to this new land they accepted that life would not be the same. That they would exchange parts of their old identity for a new one that would, in turn, unlock a sense of belonging to this new place.

My ancestors understood that the differences they had with the people around them were eclipsed by the future they would share together.

I see each line of my ancestors as its own stream, with different points of origin and bends in their journeys, coming together to form a powerful river.

1.2 *whakapapa*

A week before my sixth birthday my father died. He was forty-one. My mother, thirty-nine, was left to raise four children, aged twelve, ten, five and three.

Beyond the shock and suffering, something precious was broken. My father, an only child, was the direct link to our English and Māori ancestors. His elderly mother, my Nana Rose, lived over a thousand miles away to the north. Heartbroken herself, we would only see her every few years.

Over time, grief began to be accompanied by a sense of something stolen, a wrong that had been unjustly visited upon us. Someone who had been holding your hand had let go and it would take a very long time to grip onto that sense of belonging again.

This loss involved a violent breaking of a heritage we were born into. A sense of dislocation from a place I had never been, but where I knew I belonged.

As the years passed, a yearning to know more fed a determination to repair this broken chain.

When I was twelve, I wrote a letter to the office of *Ngāi Tahu*, our Māori tribe. I asked them, in essence, *What do you know about who I am?* I didn't really expect a reply. But I got one. I don't retain the covering letter *Ngāi Tahu* wrote back to me but I know what it said: *You belong.*

It welcomed me to my tribe. I was provided with a tribal registration number. Two documents were enclosed in the envelope. I have kept both. One was a formal record, with detailed information of my Māori genealogy. Highlighted were two matriarchs, cousins of each other, Pakinui and Tiaki Kaika, both alive in 1848. This 'legally' entitled myself and my siblings, and our children, to be classified as Māori under New Zealand law.

The other document, a scruffy single page, had no heading. It was a list of ancestors' names going back more than twenty generations. No dates, no commentary. One ancestor's name after the other down the page, finishing with my father at the bottom. The covering letter from my tribe referred to this as my 'whakapapa' (pronounced far-ka-pa-pa).

The first name, at the top of this page, was Paikea (pronounced pie-key-ah). In this one name, this one word, two worlds would collide.

Paikea was taught in schools as a mythical character, 'the whale rider' – a Māori legend. We learned that Paikea was the heir apparent to the godly Chief Uenuku, in our spiritual home-land of Hawaiki, and that his half-brother had taken him out to sea on a canoe to fish and there tried to kill him so that he could inherit the chiefdom for himself. Paikea had escaped this fate by jumping from the canoe and calling a whale, who saved him and took him to safety all the way across the Pacific Ocean to the islands we now call home.

This piece of paper was boldly saying something different. It was telling me that Paikea was a real person who I was related to. On that list he took only one line, the same space as my father.

After Paikea, came Tahu, from whom our tribe takes its name, who came to this land on the *Takitimu* canoe and named the mountains under which my mother was born.

The emptiness I carried with me slowly started to subside. I recall a feeling of euphoria upon reading this, a deep sense of belonging to something greater than myself.

Over time, I have come to understand *whakapapa* in this way:

Each of us are part of an unbreakable chain of people going back and forward in time. Back to our first ancestor at the beginning of time and into the future to the end of time. Each of us in this chain of people have our arms interlocked with those on either side of us. We are unbreakable. Together, immortal.

The sun rose in the east and shone on our first ancestor. Here is our origin story. Just as happens with each passing day, the sun slowly moves down this unbreakable chain of people. Each of us will have our time in the sun. But the sun is always moving. Moving towards the west, where it will finally settle.

When the sun shines on us we are alive, we are strong. For we have had passed down to us a culture that immerses us in deep belonging. We feel safe and respected. We share beliefs and a sense of identity with those around us and this anchors us. We share a purpose with them. We share a vision of the future. We fit in here. Rituals and traditions tie us together. The experiences and wisdom of those who walked in the light before our time are passed on to us.

Whakapapa points a finger at us and tells us, *You will not be judged by your money or celebrity or sense of self pride . . . you will be judged by what you did for our tribe.*

When the sun is shining on us, we must be guardians of our tribe and of each other.

This is how I have come to understand *whakapapa*.

Beyond kin, *whakapapa* frames our connection to any group we belong to. This reach of *whakapapa* was illustrated for me one day while having coffee with my friend Michael Campbell. In 2005 Michael became the first New Zealander to win the US Golf Open. Not only did Michael win this prestigious 'major' but he did so in epic style. After the third round he was down four shots to South African Retief Goosen but came back to overtake him and then, over the last nine holes of the tournament at Pinehurst in North Carolina, he held off Tiger Woods in a classic dual. Michael is a Māori New Zealander. As we chatted, he reflected on his achievement in this way:

> 'One of the most satisfying feelings I now have is that I am part of a *whakapapa* with other winners of this trophy like Bobby Jones, Ben Hogan, Arnold Palmer, Jack Nicklaus and Tiger. No matter what happens, that cannot change. That bond between us can never be broken.'

From the first winner, Horace Rawlins in 1895, a line of US Open champions has revealed itself. One after the other, year after year. The arms of these champions interlinked. In 2005, the sun revealed Michael as the newest member of this prestigious tribe, but he had always been there.

It is crucial to understand that *whakapapa*, like so many indigenous ideas, was gifted to us by our ancestors as a highly practical tool for us to deploy in our lives and work. It has been given to us so that we understand how to build strong tribes and strong teams.

Whakapapa is the starting point in my work with teams and

leaders. It unlocks our sense of identity. If we inherit a legacy, we extract meaning from it. If we are beginning a new venture, then we shape our genesis story with intent. Our deeds will be an expression of the identity we build.

Having spoken about *whakapapa* around the world, I have come to understand that it is a universal idea. I received a powerful affirmation of this when I was invited to work with the Command Group of the NATO military alliance based in Mons, Belgium.

The Command Group comprises the four-star generals who oversee NATO's military operations. In 2012 this included the Supreme Allied Commander for Europe Admiral Jim Stavridis from the US Navy, Deputy SACEUR General Sir Richard Shirreff of the British Army and Chief of Staff General Manfred Lange of the German Air Force.

As part of our work together we invoked *whakapapa* to reflect on previous NATO Command Groups: looking at the leadership challenges they faced when the sun shone on them and the legacies they ultimately left.

We began with the first ancestors and the genesis story. This revolved around the 1949 Treaty of Washington that formed the alliance, and the first Command Group which included General (later President) Dwight Eisenhower and his deputy, British General Bernard Montgomery. Then, through the decades, we reflected on each Command Group's 'time in the sun' and their legacy.

The generals then previewed their own legacy as the sixteenth leadership team and articulated this in writing. Sir Richard Shirreff reflected this exercise back to me:

'*Whakapapa* made a great impression on me. The notion of being part of an unbroken chain, those before us and those after us, with the sun shining on us in this moment. It particularly focused me on creating and setting conditions for success for those that would follow us.'

That sentiment towards *whakapapa* was reaffirmed the following year when I visited Mons and Admiral Stavridis' office. The centrepiece of the office is the oak desk of General (also later President) Ulysses S. Grant, which he had used during the American Civil War as leader of the Union Army. This was brought to Mons by first ancestor General Eisenhower when he took up his role. In the middle of the desk was Admiral Stavridis' computer, to the left of it a photo of his family and beside that the *whakapapa* legacy statement that he had written.

When I consider my other ancestral lines, they too have their own version of *whakapapa*. My Irish ancestral lines can be traced in the *Leabhar na nGenealach* (*Book of Genealogies*) written in the 1600s. My English ancestral lines can be pieced together before and after the *Liber de Wintonia* (*Domesday Book*) of 1086.

Our identity is a fusion of stories, myth, genealogy and personalities that we step into.

Whilst ideas like *whakapapa* are highly practical tools for us to build strong teams, they also have a powerful spiritual dimension. They explicitly connect us to something greater than ourselves.

Whakapapa counters a universal anxiety in *homo sapiens* around our own impermanence and mortality. Russian novelist Vladimir Nabokov cues *whakapapa* itself in his dark reflection that:

> *Our existence is but a brief crack of light between two eternities of darkness.*[2]

Whakapapa offers a sense of immortality. Being able to attach ourselves to something permanent in our impermanent world. A sense of continuity and stability despite the evidence of constant change and chaos around us. It provides an antidote, a source of calm. *Whakapapa* holds out a hand to a world beyond this one.

My friend Michael Gervais, a leading United States performance psychologist and host of the highly rated podcast *Finding Mastery*, sees *whakapapa* as also being an enabler of a mindful approach to both performance and life:

> 'Impermanence is a natural part of the human condition, each moment unfolding, unpredictable and expiring. *Whakapapa* encourages us to settle into the moment, locked into the people around us.'

1.3 our primal need to belong

Our ancestors deeply understood our primal need to belong, before psychology or neuroscience gathered the proof. It was visceral to them, part of every day and every decision.

From the time our human ancestors left the forests to live on the grasslands, the greatest determinant of individual survival was whether they belonged to a strong group.

On those grasslands, we carried obvious physiological disadvantages to other animals. As science writer David Berreby writes:

> It's not hard to see why humans should have evolved to care about their teams and their place on those teams. Relying on each other is a sound survival strategy for a frail, noisy creature without a lot of built-in weapons. Living in groups is a ticket to survival, which is why most primates live in them.[3]

The one true competitive advantage we found was strength in our togetherness. This was what gave us a fighting chance of survival. From this brutal reality the super strength of *homo sapiens* emerged, this ability to form strongly bonded and highly effective groups.

Isolation or rejection from a group spelled premature death – those two states still terrify the hell out of us. There has never been a time in human history when our wellbeing has not been tied to belonging to a group. Studies today reaffirm the correlation between chronic loneliness, poor health and early mortality.[4] We know that after a cardiac arrest the strength of an individual's social network is a greater predictor of survivability than exercise, nutrition or medication.[5]

We are terrified of rejection – of being judged not worthy of belonging to a particular group. Of not sharing the necessary traits or background. Of not fitting in. Of not being good enough. Of not being seen. Those who have experienced serious social rejection are over twenty times more likely to develop depression.[6]

To feel a sense of belonging is to feel accepted, to feel seen and to feel included by a group of people, believing that we fit in, trusting we will be protected by them. To not feel belonging is to experience the precarious and insecure sense of an outsider.

Historically, the family unit, our kin, has been the safest place for us. From there, we have carefully built out, in concentric circles, other safe groups to belong to. Our extended family. Those immediately around where we live, our neighbours. Working groups. The wider community we share an identity with. Tribes.

These are the people we can most trust. These are the people who will have our backs in hard times. These are the people our wellbeing is tied to.

It's why the term 'family' is perhaps overused in teams. It cues the deepest primal sense of belonging and trust. In the words of a former gang member:

'This underlying sense of belonging mirrors unbreakable bonds. There is a feeling of euphoria that I am part of something, that people look at me and I have respect. I am a something. I am a somebody. The thing I got out of it was the loyalty of another brother next to me in good times and bad.'

Feelings of insecurity over belonging trigger our fight, flight or freeze response. Our attention cascades into the present emergency. Stress hormones and adrenalin take control. Our heart races, our breath speeds up, digestion pauses, blood vessels constrict, eyes dilate. We literally tighten up. Tunnel vision takes over. Our thinking ability is reduced. Our capacity to communicate with those around us diminishes.

On the other hand, when we experience a sense of belonging our body produces a hormone soup that enables oxytocin, serotonin, dopamine and endorphins to work their collective magic. Stress hormones are still there but in balance; our anxiety and fear are lowered and we feel calmer and safer. This allows us to trust, communicate and co-operate at a higher level. Our oxytocin system makes us more empathetic to those in our group and sensitive to their approval.[7] Our serotonin system guides our mood. Our dopamine system shifts motivation from self-preservation to meeting others' expectations. Endorphins signal moments of social bonding.

Our need to belong is, therefore, not just in the mind, but a physical state. It is hardwired into our biology. When social relationships feel under threat we respond both emotionally and physically as though our survival is threatened. The same area in our brain is engaged as if we were suffering physical pain.[8] It is an example of how our biology has adapted an ancient system in order to drive our need to belong.

Our senses are primed to constantly seek information about belonging from our environment. We are hardwired to quickly and intuitively understand whether or not we are in a safe place with people we can trust. Our anxiety system is permanently tuned into this question. Hormones are released to instantaneously give feedback on relative levels of comfort and fear in our surroundings.

In *The Culture Code*, Dan Coyle cites the work of the Massachusetts Institute of Technology's Human Dynamics Lab in investigating micro belonging cues. Alongside words spoken, we place significant weight on largely unconscious physical signals in social settings: proximity, eye contact, body language, turn-taking, vocal pitch and conversation flow.[9]

One of cricket's great players today, AB de Villiers, captured it in this way for me:

'There is always uncertainty and insecurity coming into any new team. It was that way growing up and remains the same even at elite level. On my first day in a new team I can feel whether this is a safe place for me or not, whether I belong there.'

Belonging is never a state that is permanently achieved. It is something we continually monitor and evaluate. Consistency in environment and the behaviour of those around us are key. Ambiguity or mixed signalling seriously elevate anxiety.

Performing at something that is important to us involves stress. The question is whether our hormone blend is enabling motivation, engagement and focus, or disabling us through distraction, wasted energy and disconnection from teammates.

Our ancestors fully understood this causal relationship between our environment and our sense of belonging. This is why they tried to help us with ideas such as *whakapapa*.

The science is catching up with them.

1.4 leakage

Belonging is a wildly undervalued condition required for human performance.

When our need to belong in a team is met, our energy and focus pour into the team's shared mission. We can lock into our role and the tasks we're being asked to deliver. We are comfortable being vulnerable in our quest to get better. We feel secure enough to help others and point out where we could be better as a team.

We can be ourselves. We feel that we are respected and that we matter. We feel included. We can be a good teammate here. Our own identity and that of the team happily coexist.

We are tuned into the legacy we're about to write.

We feel like Yuhui Choe. Yuhui is a third-generation Korean raised in Japan. She left home at fourteen to study ballet in Paris. By eighteen she had won prestigious international competitions and become an apprentice at the Royal Ballet in London's Covent Garden. Yuhui is now first soloist there.

In her dance, Yuhui brings her own rich identity to that of the quintessential English institution that is the Royal Ballet:

'I always apply my ideas from the Japanese and Korean cultures. Japanese zen moments when things are not going right – step back and think. Korean – *ma-eun* is the word

26

I like – is more passionate about what we love and can be loud, like fireworks.'

This is the world of belonging.

But there is another world, maybe more commonplace, where the hormone soup recipe is wrong and doesn't allow for us to be at our best.

If our need to belong is unmet, we leak energy and focus by obsessing on the unsafe environment and relations around us. There is no performance benefit in that.

Someone who has felt a sense of not belonging, of exclusion, is international women's football player Ali Riley. After graduating with a psychology degree from Stanford University, she has played professionally in the United States, Sweden, England and Germany. Amidst much success and acclaim, Ali has also had experiences where she has felt excluded. These are the emotional low points of her career:

'When you feel excluded you feel your purpose has been taken away. To not be looked in the eye, not spoken to directly, wondering if it is personal; feeling lost, confused. You feel that you have no control. When you are alone with your thoughts, especially at night, it all comes back as you get ready for the next day when it will all happen again.'

Our energy and focus are absorbed by the infinite calculations our brain has to make to navigate each social situation with our leaders and teammates. In every interaction we feel judged and pressure builds. This takes our focus away from the step-by-step process of preparing and performing at our best.

Our thinking capacity and ability to evaluate risk diminish. Our working memory is interrupted by the noise of negative belonging cues. We struggle to toggle between tasks. We may become more aggressive, though we are likely to target that at those we perceive as having lower status than us.

We may struggle to trust those around us as relationships feel transactional. We have a growing sense that others might not have our backs if things don't go well. We fear that what we disclose may be used against us.

A paradox plays out. We are preoccupied with fitting in and being accepted yet we become withdrawn. We minimise what we perceive as moments of vulnerability with others. We have decided that it's safer to stay in the shadows. We avoid speaking up, let alone taking any responsibility. We know this is detrimental to our learning and development, but we offset it by reducing our risk of exclusion. We become a poorer teammate – not because of a flaw in our character but because we feel unsafe and threatened.

We are in self-preservation mode and the fate of the team becomes a secondary consideration. Our mind prioritises what we need to do to survive here, over what the team needs to do to succeed.

In early 2018 I was working with the South African cricket team when they played Australia at home in a highly controversial series. An infamous moment transpired during the third day of the third test. One of Australia's least experienced players, Cameron Bancroft, was shown on television (and on screens around the ground) illegally rubbing the ball with a small object, which later turned out to be sandpaper.

This was a blatant breach of the spirit and laws of the game.

After an initial denial of wrongdoing, over the following days it transpired that Cameron had been directed to do this by the team's vice captain and captain – his leaders. All three players were subsequently given lengthy bans from the game.

What particularly interested me was Cameron's motivation to break the rules. So many people had come out in public to say what a good man he was and how what he had done was out of character. Nowhere in the media coverage did I see Cameron's need to belong mentioned. However, a hint of that contributing factor comes from a largely overlooked remark he made:

'I didn't know any better because I just wanted to fit in and feel valued really. As simple as that . . . what I valued at the time – I valued fitting in.'[10]

As is so often the case, this unmet need to belong led directly to failure. Here, Cameron's need for approval and inclusion resulted in expulsion from the sport he loved and the team he'd dreamed of being part of.

How much talent have we wasted by undervaluing our primal need to belong?

1.5 two worlds of belonging

It all started with the Industrial Revolution.

In the north of England in the 1800s a radical shift emerged in the way humans worked. We moved from workers possessing multiple skills and dynamically performing multiple tasks, to production lines where rows of workers each performed a distinct role.

The role of management was to oversee this process and ensure each person performed their isolated task – and if they didn't, replace them with someone who would. If there was a production error, then the fault, or culprit, could be isolated and fixed.

A leading management voice at the turn of the twentieth century was American Frederick Winslow Taylor. Taylor wrote the highly influential *The Principles of Scientific Management* which espoused industrial efficiency. In his book Taylor declared: *In the past the man has been first; in the future the system must be first.*[11]

Lost in this transformation in the way we work was part of our humanity and I would argue we have yet to fully regain it.

Our ancient ancestors' wisdom on teams did not seem to fit into this new world of working. We became disconnected from each other. Our value became individualised. We became silos.

At the same time as we revolutionised working practices modern sport emerged. From the start, this production-line mindset infiltrated the coaching of sport. In football and baseball, it is no coincidence that today the coach is still known as 'the manager'.

The role of the production manager was to ensure the workplace was as efficient and productive as possible. That the technical pieces were in place, that the operation was organised, that each person performed a specific role, and all of this was statistically measured.

There is an inherent problem with this. Most high-performing team activities are nothing like linear production lines. Team performance is not an aggregation of individual tasks being completed. Our contribution is hugely influenced by the acts of others, such as an opponent actively seeking to disrupt us, and a range of random events beyond anyone's control.

Here, our ancient ancestors' wisdom is timeless. Success is dependent on the strength of the group under pressure. In order to stay strong, aligned and cohesive we have evolved needs that must be met – starting with our need to belong.

This production line mindset pervades working environments today. It is not just with management either. Stakeholders, media and the public look at performance in the same way. When results are not as desired there is a reflex that an individual deemed responsible be identified and replaced so that the illusory linear process of winning can be 'fixed'.

Former England football star Michael Owen is someone with deep insight into how our need to belong plays out in football.

I first met Michael in 2016 when I was appointed by the English Football Association to help strengthen the team culture of their national teams. I started this work by immersing myself into the culture (and *whakapapa*) of the England men's football team. Michael was one of the former England players I spoke with.

In the course of our chats over the years, Michael has shared a powerful illustration of the contrasts between a met and an unmet need to belong. Specifically, his contrasting experiences at first Liverpool Football Club in England and then at Real Madrid in Spain.

At Liverpool, Michael played through the youth system at the club, making his senior debut at seventeen. He went on to play for Liverpool for eight years, scoring 158 goals in 297 games. Michael explained to me the strong sense of belonging he had at Liverpool:

'Everyone knew me as a person, not just as a player. I felt part of the inner sanctum of the club. I had a deep affinity with the fans. The manager (Gérard Houllier) knew mine and my wife's families and he would go over and speak with them after games. It was a safe environment. I could relax and get on with the job. I was able to mentally cope more easily in that environment.'

Michael's description is echoed in the club's anthem 'You'll never walk alone', which itself captures the very essence of belonging.

In 2004 Michael transferred to Real Madrid. This team, known as the 'Galácticos', included a host of world-class players including Zinedine Zidane, Raúl, (Brazilian) Ronaldo, Luís Figo, Roberto Carlos, David Beckham and Iker Casillas. Although playing well (scoring thirteen goals in thirty-six appearances in La Liga), Michael never fully settled at the club, nor did he unleash his full potential. He returned to England at the end of a single season.

Talent wasn't the issue. Just a few seasons before Michael had won the Ballon d'Or (Golden Ball) award, the most prestigious individual award for football players in the world.

Here are Michael's words on what it felt like joining Real Madrid:

'When you arrive, there are a lot of thoughts floating around. Am I going to be accepted by the other players? Who will I get on with? Will the manager like me? Will my style of play fit? Will the fans take to me? When will my first goal come? How will the egos in the dressing room play out? None of those questions I thought about at Liverpool. I was a mentally strong player, but if you had any self-doubt, you had no chance.'

Michael then directly addresses his need to belong:

'I felt I belonged from a talent point of view, but I felt less confident in the social space of the team. Of all those things, the most important was getting the respect of my team-mates and being accepted by that dressing room. I wanted to be the player they trusted to give the ball to in the big moments of the games. As a result, I struggled to assert my personality and allow them to get to know me as a person. I went from a prankster in the Liverpool dressing room to feeling a little like an outsider.'

Although these are personal reflections, they represent universal feelings that are hardwired into all of us.

These deep-seated emotions were met by a mechanical approach: a focus on accumulating talent, organising it and managing it. Michael was introduced as a new signing at the Bernabéu Stadium in Madrid in front of twenty-five thousand fans and then . . . nothing.

No induction. No welcome. No personal conversation with the manager or a club leader to explain this new tribe he had joined or how they saw his place in it. Instead, Michael went straight into technical meetings and squad training. The unspoken message was clear: prove yourself and then you can belong here.

Real Madrid is the most successful club in European football history. The tribe with the most external status. It was a complex dressing room: high talent, big egos, a huge diversity of characters. But no space was created to connect Michael Owen with his new team. No story provided to attach a sense of belonging to. No proactive measures taken to connect him and his new teammates.

In Māori culture, a word for leader is *rangatira*, which itself consists of two words – *raranga*, meaning to weave, and *tira*, meaning a group, so *rangatira* literally means 'to weave a group of people together'.[12] At Real Madrid, *rangatira* was missing.

Michael's differing mindset in these two contrasting environments was completely natural. They were not quirks of his personality but logical responses triggered by how we are all wired to feel and think in teams.

Our ancestors would shake their heads at this: compromising talent is not part of our evolutionary story. They shared their experience and wisdom with us, but we thought we knew better.

1.6 making it personal

I know many performers who waited for belonging cues that never came. They met up with the team, they were kitted out, they were taught the team's tactical language, they trained with their new team, they ate and travelled together. All the time, feeling like an outsider, maybe even an imposter. They talk of the heavy weight of not feeling a sense of belonging as they were sent out to compete in front of millions.

Many of us have had a similar experience in a corporate working context. We are inducted into processes but not the tribe. We begin our work, navigating the myriad relationships involved, having a sense of being judged and needing to prove ourselves in every exchange. Wanting desperately to fit in. A sense of belonging to something that may exist in the future, if we survive. Somehow, we are expected to exhibit the best of our talent as this plays out.

The Royal Marines know better than this.

I have come to learn a little about the way the Royal Marines do things through my friendship with retired major Scotty Mills. We met when we were both helping Gareth Southgate and the England football team prepare for the 2018 FIFA World Cup in Russia.

Scotty went from being one of the few black recruits in the

1980s to becoming the highest-ranking commissioned black officer in Royal Marines history. In his career, Scotty served in war zones in Northern Ireland, Iraq and Helmand Province in Afghanistan. He later became Head of Physical Training and Performance at the Royal Marines Commando Training Centre at Lympstone on the south coast of England.

In late 2018, Scotty invited me to the graduation ceremony for new Marines that follows thirty-two weeks' brutal Commando training. This is where the iconic green berets are presented.

What particularly struck me about the green beret presentation was the deeply personal way it was conducted.

The Royal Marines had learned from their own ancestors that this ceremony provided a critical opportunity to instil a deep sense of belonging. An awareness that we retain the emotional feeling of a first experience much longer than the details of the encounter.

I had been expecting formality and pageantry. Instead, the green beret ceremony was intimate, deeply personalised and full of humour. The formalities were much more background than foreground.

On stage, in an auditorium within the Royal Marines' training base at Lympstone, stood the presiding officers along with the graduating class themselves, known as the King's Squad.

The audience was full of family members across the generations, from babies to grandparents. It was noisy – babies crying, kids talking – and it stayed that way throughout the hour-long ceremony. Rather than feeling discomfort, it was clear that the presiding officers embraced this atmosphere. They connected immediately with the audience by highlighting a few family members' birthdays as well as identifying former Royal Marines present.

The message was clear – *We are kin, and everyone belongs here.*

This point was reinforced in the opening address – the idea of the 'corps family'. The presiding officer went one step further, in expressly telling the families in the audience that they had also joined the Royal Marines that day.

The 'corps family' was an expression I had heard Scotty use a number of times. What struck me as particularly authentic about that belonging phrase was a passing comment Scotty had made that in his thirty-two years as a Royal Marine he had never experienced one incident of discrimination or racial abuse: 'The only time I ever notice my skin colour is darker is when I look into the mirror to shave.'

Scotty shared with me that in his own green beret presentation ceremony in 1987 his close family was present with one addition . . . a great-uncle, who he had never met up to that point, who joined them that day, sitting there holding his own green beret from the Second World War.

At the ceremony that I attended, each of the new Commandos were individually introduced. Each receiving a personal and humorous remark as they were handed their green beret.

After the presentation of the green berets the King's Squad relocated to the parade ground and the traditional passing out parade took place. Here was the pageantry that I had been anticipating.

At the end of the parade, something caught my attention. To the side of the parade ground was a long corrugated-iron shed. I asked Scotty if I could take a look in it. Inside the shed, hanging from the four walls, were photos of each graduating Commando class through the years.

A line of unbroken ancestors, and space for the next generation to step into the light.

Whakapapa.

1.7 belonging for all

*Difference can be the seabed of our delight with each
other rather than something that has to be colonised.*
Irish poet and conflict mediator Pádraig Ó Tuama[13]

One of the ways in which a sense of belonging is engendered in
my country is through the 'All Blacks', our national rugby team.

The All Blacks have won four out of every five matches they've
played since the 1890s. They continue to bring us pride and
confidence. This sustained level of high performance over such a
long period defies easy explanation. It has gone on too long, and
been too consistent, to attribute to a few key individuals. The All
Blacks have never had any obvious competitive advantage over
other nations in terms of playing numbers or economics.

Iconic All Black Zinzan Brooke, who played one hundred
games for the team including its first World Cup win, identifies
team culture as the critical source of this competitive advantage:

'If it is not because of the money or players, how do New
Zealand consistently set the bar so high? In my opinion, it
is because of the culture ... Every year people who wear
that shirt create history and leave a benchmark for the next
generation to aspire to.'[14]

39

Whakapapa.

The All Blacks certainly have an uncommon awareness of the impact of their environment on their performance. This reflects the deep diversity that has always existed in the team in terms of race, religion, education and occupation. This, in turn, has required particular attention to ensure togetherness and trust. There has never been a time when that could be taken for granted.

Winning 80 per cent of matches over 130 years could imply a successful template was found early on and then reproduced generation after generation. However, that is not the case. In fact, the All Blacks have continually reinvented their culture over time as they have adapted to changes in context.

The All Blacks' World Cup wins in 2011 and 2015 coincided with another period of cultural renewal in the team. In the words of former All Blacks captain Anton Oliver:

> 'There have been many reasons given for this period of All Black domination over the last decade or more, but right at the top of them is belonging and a freedom to express your own sense of identity that comes with that.'

Renewal is fundamental to *whakapapa*. The sun is always moving. Nothing is new, yet everything is new. There is only ever a moment in time, nothing can be done exactly the same way twice. As *Ngāi Tahu* artist Simon Kaan puts it, using a surfing metaphor:

> 'When you're on a wave there is a moment in time that can't be recreated. So, you have to be right in the moment and

respond to that situation in a way that's familiar because you've done it thousands of times, but each time is new again.'[15]

Whakapapa demands that each generation has an obligation as cultural guardians not to preserve the status quo but to strengthen it. Hence the team's ethos *leave the shirt in a better place.*

In this way, *whakapapa* can be seen as an expression of the theory of evolution itself – a necessity to adapt to changing external conditions in order to survive. Continually finding new ways to ensure the efficient transmission of experiences, lessons and wisdom down the chain of people.

Anton Oliver was a witness to this period of renewal. Over his thirteen seasons in the All Blacks he saw the culture evolve by expanding the cues of belonging it sent to an increasingly diverse team.

Anton started his All Black career in 1995, a time when rugby was transitioning from an amateur game to today's fully professional sport. Within the team, this transition played out culturally. The old ways had brought a lot of success but the new players arriving in the team were different. They were generally younger and came from more diverse backgrounds than before.

Joining the All Blacks as a nineteen-year-old, Anton initially struggled to settle:

'It was a "my jersey" culture back then where junior players were expected to keep their heads down and mouths shut. I was in the All Blacks but not – true acceptance was only obtained through getting on the field and performing well, which could take years before one got the opportunity: years of feeling excluded.'

Anton describes a culture where the established senior players had a deep sense of belonging and connection with each other, but others felt excluded from this inner sanctum. He notes that this was not intended but was symptomatic of the culture that had been passed down to them from a more hierarchical society of earlier generations. However, from Anton's point of view it was not the way to get the best out of everyone: 'I felt conditional acceptance, second class, excluded.'

A colonisation of belonging by an established few who enjoy status and power is common across groups and teams. Often, those pockets of power come from a dominant clique (status, class, gender, race, religion, education, schooling) and their view of the world becomes the default setting for the group.

Anton himself had a particular sensitivity to belonging cues. From a young age he'd suffered from social anxiety. Looking back, he connects this to a few things. He was always physically bigger than other kids, his size a source of teasing. He couldn't help attracting unwanted attention. He yearned to fit in. He recalls the humiliation of starting a new school and on the first day not being able to fit his legs under the desk and having to be relocated to a mat.

Anton also connects his social anxiety to his father leaving him, his mother and two brothers when he was three, and moving away to start a new family:

'A sense of belonging was a particularly big deal for me. On reflection, it's something I'd always struggled with but have only gained any kind of understanding of in the last few years. The young me felt a deep sense of abandonment and rejection. As a consequence, I've always coveted belonging to a group and been very sensitive to any type of rejection.'

In 2004, after a loss of form on the field and behavioural issues, the All Blacks' leadership pressed the pause button. They concluded that the All Blacks' culture needed to change. It had emerged out of a more hierarchical Anglo-Saxon dominated society of earlier generations. However, it needed to evolve to get the best out of their increasingly diverse playing group.

Between 1890 and 1990, 90 per cent of All Blacks were 'white' (of European descent). Today, they represent 40 per cent of the team, with Polynesians in the majority.[16]

Underpinning this period of renewal was a more inclusive definition of what belonging meant in the team. A powerful message was delivered to all the players: *You belong here whatever your personal story and own sense of identity.* Anton describes the shift in this way:

'Think of the All Blacks today as a borderless platform that allows far greater flexibility for individuals to plug in their own sense of belonging and meaning.'

In order for this more inclusive approach to emerge it needed to be accompanied by greater cultural awareness within the team. This required some courageous and highly intentional leadership.

Sessions were held where each of the ethnic groups explained to the rest of the team the core beliefs of their culture. Wayne Smith, one of the All Blacks' coaches at the time, reflected:

'We got the [Māori], Fijians, Samoans, Tongans and Europeans to speak, and it was amazing to hear the differences in attitudes ... totally different mental models and value systems ... The attitudes of [European] to Polynesian players in the team have changed ... there's much more understanding of their values, who they are and where they come from, and that's been positive in the group ... that's come about through acknowledgement, working to overcome it, rather than just ignoring it.'[17]

Jerome Kaino was a key member of the All Blacks between 2004 and 2017, finishing his career with two World Cup winners' medals. Jerome was born in American Samoa and moved with his family to New Zealand when he was four. As with a number of other players in the team, while Jerome was raised in New Zealand his Pacific culture, language and way of life dominated at home. Jerome described himself to me as 'Samoan first and proud New Zealander second'.

Jerome recalls that what he took away, above all else, from the team culture sharing sessions was that the common bond among them was the primacy of family, of kin. A safe place where love was unconditional, and trust was high. He says it became a collective aspiration to replicate that in the All Blacks' environment.

Jerome arrived in the team in 2004, precisely when this cultural renewal was taking place. He explained to me that coming into the team as a 'rookie', he expected some reservation from established players until he had proven himself, just as Anton had experienced a decade before. However, that was not the case. Instead, Jerome found, from the outset, senior players proactively approaching him, welcoming him to the team and involving him in team life. This varied from simply coming over and sitting with him at meals through to asking for his views in team meetings.

These belonging cues were taken to another level when Jerome went through the long-standing induction rituals of the All Blacks and was presented with his shirt the night before his debut and then asked to speak to the team in the dressing room after his first match. Wayne Smith has described the All Blacks' induction process in pure *whakapapa* terms:

> 'We have an induction into the All Blacks' legacy: what it means, what the All Blacks have achieved, what they've been about for over 110 years, what standards are expected, the need to establish your own legacy. When you're handed your jersey, you understand you are only in it for a short time and your responsibility is to hand it on and for it to be better than it was before you got it.'[18]

Other belonging rituals included new All Blacks being taken into the boardroom and shown each team photo from 1893 to the present day. Senior players providing ritualised questions, with the new players sharing their answers with the team.[19] Senior players telling the All Blacks' identity story to new players.[20] A black book provided to new players setting out the All Blacks' identity story and cultural framework.

Rituals can have real power in embedding a deep sense of belonging. The induction is the most critical time as an individual has their mind most open to this new experience. They are in a highly receptive state that enables them to learn about their new tribe and absorb its beliefs and values. Our first experiences have a long-lasting impact on our sense of being part of this team. The undertaking of rituals also facilitates an emotional connection to new team members that further deepens belonging, reduces anxiety and enhances the conditions for deep trust.

It is important that rituals and traditions have a presence beyond the induction of new members. These not only refresh an individual's own sense of belonging but keep everyone connected to the collective sense of identity and 'tribal' beliefs. These may include a ritual to commence a new 'campaign', closure on certain events or 'chapters', and rites of passage events such as milestones and, importantly, beloved members transitioning out of the team.

The All Blacks' quest for authentic inclusiveness was not just about rituals, though. It was embedded into the weekly structure and rhythm of how the team operated.

Small groups within the team were formed to give voice to every player. There were unit groups where all players were expected to contribute. A new players' group was set up, facilitated by a senior player, to listen to the rookies' views on anything they wanted to discuss. Ideas from this group were funnelled up to team leadership and led directly to further progressive changes.

Deploying smaller groups to facilitate each player finding their voice works particularly well when young players come from highly hierarchical communities. For them, the default is to fully respect authority and not speak up, let alone challenge what their 'elders' are doing or saying. Deploying small groups is a way of disrupting that reluctance to articulate. Over time, individuals find their voice in those small groups and gain confidence to share their thoughts in the wider team space.

Crucially, during this time of renewal, the All Blacks refreshed their own identity story.

While the national team first played in 1893, the first team known as the 'All Blacks' was the 1905 team that toured the United Kingdom, France and North America. This team has become known as the 'Originals'. They were captained by Dave Gallaher who, over time, has become regarded as a father figure of the All Blacks.

On that 1905 tour the All Blacks played thirty-five matches, winning thirty-four. That success adds to Gallaher's place as a particularly powerful ancestor. A migrant (from Ireland), prior to becoming an All Black in 1903, he voluntarily enlisted in the New Zealand Mounted Rifles and fought in the Boer War in South Africa. He rose through the ranks to become an officer.

In 1916, aged forty-two, Gallaher enlisted to fight in the First World War after his brother was killed in France. He was too old to have been conscripted, twice the age of many other soldiers, but he volunteered out of a sense of duty. Gallaher fought in the Battle of Messines (an iconic battle for New Zealanders) and then, on 4 October 1917, aged forty-three, was killed at Gravenstafel Spur on the first day of the Battle of Passchendaele.

As part of this reconnection to its *whakapapa*, the All Blacks visited Dave Gallaher's place of birth in County Donegal in Ireland. The following year, they visited his gravesite at Nine Elms cemetery in Belgium before their test match against France.

Gallaher's gravesite reconnected the team with the 1924 All

Blacks team, the 'Invincibles' (who won all thirty-six matches on their tour). They were the first team to visit Gallaher's gravesite on 7 January 1925. Poignantly, half of that All Blacks team had themselves fought in the First World War. Several of them had fought in Passchendaele. One of them, Les Cupples, was awarded the Military Medal for bravery in recovering fallen soldiers in the same field where Gallaher fell.

Layers upon layers.

Anton himself presented stories of the All Blacks in the Great War to the team before their test match against France in 2006. In Anton's words:

'The work we did with the 1905 Originals hugely increased my own sense of belonging. I couldn't believe we'd never done it before. Connecting to the Originals in this way felt like we were connecting with our ancestors and immediately created the sense of a continuum through time – one which spanned over 100 years. It was a hugely powerful and emotional moment. It created a deep focus on what our legacy will be.'

This reconnection was also significant for Jerome Kaino:

'The team's *whakapapa* gave the jersey deeper meaning for me. Learning about Dave Gallaher, the Invincibles, those who fought in the wars, Polynesian All Blacks. *Whakapapa* intertwines the Māori and Samoan cultures, which are very similar, and New Zealand as a nation. This is my identity. There is no meaning imposed. It is for you to give it yourself.'

Whakapapa wove the All Blacks together, creating an inclusive and highly personal sense of belonging bound to a shared future they all had a stake in.

The most successful period of All Blacks rugby followed.

2

Us

If you own your memory – you can own your future.
Sir Tipene O'Regan (*Ngāi Tahu* leader)

2.1 our story back and forward

A few years after I received the first envelope from my tribe, I received another. This one unprompted. There was no covering note or letter of any sort. Instead, enclosed were pages about one of my ancestors. Her name was Pakinui, the daughter of Titope and Makahi.

Pakinui is my grandmother of five generations ago. The pages set out an outline of her life.

Pakinui was of chiefly blood, a direct descendant of Tahu, the founder of our tribe. She had a *moko* (traditional tattoo) marked into her chin, reflecting the high status of her ancestral lines.

One morning in 1832, the fortified village that eight-year-old Pakinui lived in was set alight and attacked by a great northern chief and his warriors. A terrible massacre took place. Of the thousand members of our tribe who lived in the fortified village, six hundred were killed that day.[21] Other kin were taken prisoners, made slaves and shipped to the north. A few managed to escape, including a brave girl by the name of Pakinui. She had scaled the walls at the rear of the village and trudged through swamps to safety.

This ancestor, a matriarch in our family, Pakinui, had fled as a refugee in her own land, terrorised by northern warriors. Together with the other survivors, she made her way deeper into the south. There, the refugees made new homes based on

53

the ebb and flow of the seasons and the availability of resources. They positioned themselves close to newly established European whaling stations who they could trade with. It was there that Pakinui saw white people for the first time.

In 1836, when Pakinui was twelve, there was a measles epidemic. This disease was brought by the Europeans and the indigenous people had no immunity. They were decimated, one third died. Pakinui, however, survived.

At fifteen, Pakinui became pregnant to one of those European whalers and had a son, Tomati Paraune.

Two years later she had another son, Tepene, to another European whaler.

In the next decade of Pakinui's life, these resettled refugees were evicted from the new home they had established and watched as it was handed over to European settlers. Driven out again.

I then read how Pakinui's story swept back upon itself. How, years later, she returned to that home by marrying one of the British settlers, my ancestor William Harpur. They made their own kin of eight children. We followed three generations after them.

My tribe laid out Pakinui's story for me. It was matter of fact, without interpretation.

What I understood, even at that young age, was that Pakinui was a symbol of Us.

2.2 Us and Them

Storytelling fuels the super strength of *homo sapiens* – our ability to form tightly bound groups.

Stories of Us explain our shared identity and describe for us the type of person you need to be to be part of our tribe. Eighty per cent of stories in modern hunter-gatherer societies are about how people should behave in the tribe.[22]

This sense of shared identity that underpins groups is shaped by the binary way in which *homo sapiens* see the world: Us and Them.

In order to feel deep belonging to Us, there has to be a Them.

There is an evolutionary logic to this – survival. We are safest inside the circle of Us: our family, our kin, our tribe.

For most of our evolutionary story, Them represented, in our minds at least, a form of threat – of potential violence, of disease, of outcompeting us for resources, of diminishing our status. In Them, we project people more threatening, more primitive in their ways, less intelligent and less hygienic.

In Us we see wiser, more moral, more trustworthy people. Our empathy flows more freely, in contrast to our reaction to Them. In the words of science writer David Berreby:

Alien nations, other tribes, other religions – they refuse to eat the perfectly good things we eat; they won't let their kids do the perfectly healthy things that ours do; they talk funny and their history is a childish fantasy. But us? Our tradition? That's different. The foods we avoid are unhealthy; we raise our kids right; our dialect is beautiful. And our noble history? All true![23]

Our hardwired threat sensing system starts with identifying which tribe others fall into. This is as automated in us as breathing. We see someone, we classify them as Us or Them and we then decide how to react.[24] Our fast assessments are reinforced by a bundle of inbuilt biases.

As an extension of this inbuilt radar, an uncomfortable truth is that when we see difference, our automatic and unconscious internal stress system is activated within fifty milliseconds.[25] Seconds later, the reasoning regions of our brain get an opportunity to confirm or deny this reflex anxiety. Depending on the belief system we have developed over our lives, our prejudgement will either dissolve away or stick.

From these largely unconscious calculations we create labels and metaphorically slap them on the person in front of us. There's no getting around it, this is a system that is based on prejudging and discriminating.

The evolutionary rationale is obvious enough: we had to be able to quickly detect danger. Survival was going to be seriously compromised if we had to carry out full due diligence on every new person we met.

So, we've ended up with a flawed Them evaluation system that plays out in contemporary contexts which, for most of us, bare little relation to those they were evolutionarily built for.

This dark side has, in the words of one of my heroes, Robert

Sapolsky, Professor of Biology and Neurological Sciences at Stanford University and author of *Behave*, had serious consequences:

From massive, breath-taking barbarity to countless pinpricks of microaggression, Us versus Them has produced oceans of pain.[26]

This binary way of interpreting the world remains embedded within us. However, today we are more aware of these patterns and have been able to devise effective ways to reject prejudging others by what 'tribe' we initially perceive they belong to. That remains a major work in progress for our species.

Our innate competitiveness is shaped by seeing the world as Us and Them. When we hear our beliefs replayed to us, we experience a rush of dopamine. When we hear beliefs we don't agree with, stress hormones are released.[27] We have a strong hormonal reaction to not only hearing our Us stories but also in just seeing symbols of Us (like flags and uniforms).[28] We receive dopamine hits not just when Us do well but when Them fail.[29]

Of course, most of us are able to overcome initial labelling and engage reasonably with those we perceive as different to Us. In fact, every day Us and Them fuse into new groups. Pakinui was the first Polynesian in my *whakapapa* to marry a European and have mixed-race children.

We are pragmatic and highly strategic in how we toggle between Us and Them. I grew up in a place where traditional schools were delineated between Catholics and Protestants. Rivalry, name-calling and suspicion a constant in our small-town lives. But then a regional sports team would be selected, and we would come together as a unified tribe. The new Them was that horrible region to the north of us. Now, the Catholics and Protestants became Us and the northern province became Them.

Most nations, of course, are an Us built from a diverse range of Thems. More and more people are, like me, a personification of diversity.

In building strong teams, leaders need to understand that people are highly tuned to receive the story of Us.

Herein lies an opportunity for leaders to connect with and influence teams at a deeper level.

Great leaders widen the Us story so that every person in their group feels a genuine sense of belonging. Nobody feels like an outsider or that their personal identity is devalued.

Over time, the communal telling of our tribal Us story has transferred from the campfire to churches, temples, cinemas and now other screens. But it has never left us.

I'm reminded of this each November in the Cotswolds town I live in, Chipping Campden. On Remembrance Sunday, when the nation commemorates the end of the First World War, an emotionally charged part of our village's own Us story is retold. St James' Church in the heart of the village is standing room only on this day. The horror of war is acknowledged and then deeply personalised by the reading of the names of those from our village killed across both world wars. Familiar names that still appear today in class lists and across shops in the village. Us. Our vicar's sermon wraps us in a sense of shared loss and pride. An unsaid sense sits around us that we are good people who do the right thing. Together, we ritually sing hymns and chant lines from prayers, bound less by religious beliefs and more by a need to feel part of each other. The 'Last Post' is played.

The village feels very different on this day. A fleeting sense of oneness puts its arms around us.

2.3 the campfire

Once language emerged, we congregated around the campfire at night for the telling and sharing of our Us story. This promoted our survival by keeping the group bonded together and aligned in the face of surrounding challenges.

A biological magic occurs when we share this experience. Our stress levels reduce, our sense of belonging and togetherness rise, fuelled by endorphins and oxytocin. Our dopamine system kicks in, motivating us to pursue a shared mission. It feels warm around the fire.

The tribe is its stories.

Our tribes have always given high esteem to those who carry our culture through storytelling. Whilst we often associate stories today with books, for 99 per cent of human history there was only oral storytelling. In my own culture, it was not unheard of for ancestors to be able to recite *whakapapa* across two thousand names along with their legacy stories.[30]

The nocturnal dimension of storytelling is important. Storytelling in the day centres on the practicalities of how we work together. In contrast, the stories we tell at night intimately reinforce our shared identity and serve to regulate our behaviour.[31]

Researchers, such as Joseph Campbell (*The Hero's Journey*) and Christopher Booker (*The Seven Basic Plots*), have shown us how across all ages and all cultures there are universal patterns in *homo sapiens'* storytelling.

Inside these Us stories sit a set of instructions for how to be a strong team.

The heroes in our stories personify the best version of Us. They are selfless. They serve others. They protect Us. They make Us safer. They make Us more respected in the eyes of Them. They advance our cause.

The villains fall into two camps. Them, of course. But also, the individuals within Us who are selfish. Those who put themselves before Us and thereby risk our safety, stability and status.

Our stories paint a clear picture of what is expected of Us – the collective always comes first.

The timelessness of our need for storytelling was brought home to me a few years ago when I was working with the Scotland rugby team.

I reached out to historian Katie Stevenson at St Andrews University as part of preparing for a team camp before a Six Nations Championship. I explained to Katie that, under head coach Vern Cotter's guidance, we had been reconstructing the team's Us story.

I regard this work as a sacred task. It involves immersing yourself in three dimensions of an Us story: the past, the present and the future.

I reconnect to the *past*. This requires fully immersing myself in the heritage of a team and the tribe they represent. It is typical for me to spend months researching this and most impactfully meeting 'ancestors' to hear the Us story through them. With Scotland, this involved speaking with wise elders such as Ian McGeechan, Andy Irvine and Jim Telfer. I construct a *whakapapa* of the team – including key ancestors, moments and legacies. Alongside this work I look at the wider story of the tribe the team represents – in this case the Scottish nation. This involves understanding the arc of the national Us story.

I then connect to the *future*. What is the team's vision for the next chapter of its Us story? This informs us what we are working towards and what the environment needs to enable and drive.

Finally, we focus on the *present*. Do we have a sense of identity that flows into everything we do? Do we see ourselves as part of an unbroken chain from our ancestors to those that follow us? More often than not, this needs mending.

What emerged in this work with Scotland was a strong sense of identity symbolised by the thistle (the team's emblem worn on the shirt) and anchored in the Scottish warrior archetype.

To deepen this work, I asked Katie if she could shed light on Scotland's iconic medieval warrior ancestors. I was particularly interested in how they prepared for battles.

Katie referenced the famous victory by Robert the Bruce's army over English King Edward II's army at the Battle of Bannockburn on 23–24 June 1314.

She explained that the medieval armies of the time included poets whose job it was to record events and shape the Us story that would be told afterwards. Fortunately, some of those accounts survive today.

What Katie came back with blew us away. The similarities between how the ancient warriors prepared for battle and how the nation's rugby team prepared for international matches today were striking.

Both sets of warriors – seven hundred years apart – would come into camp, near a castle, at least a week before battle. They would be welcomed, and the mission would be explained to them by their leaders. The first few days in camp would be spent practising their skills. As the week progressed, preparation moved to formations and tactics.

Both sets of warriors would be 'coached'. In Katie's words, the ancient warriors would:

'. . . gather together to discuss their strategies, to make sure they understood the vital importance not just of the goal of winning, but of being resilient under pressure, of undermining and interrupting their opponents and creating chaos to their efforts, and, most importantly, of working together as brothers . . .'

These words could easily be substituted for a team talk today.

What had a particularly eery resonance were the words 'creating chaos'. This was the famed tactic of Robert the Bruce in overcoming the numerically superior English – and it's the same language the Scotland rugby team used seven hundred years later to describe its own underdog tactics.

Clues such as this strongly affirm an authentic and deep sense of identity.

Katie relayed how the King and the army commanders would gather in the evenings before battle. They would tell stories to focus their minds on the battle the next day. This would start with classic tales, such as Alexander the Great, King Arthur, Charlemagne, and then move on to the stories of their own ancestors' victories and adventures. Then, they would talk about their own experiences. The King would invite his men to share their own stories and perspectives. These commanders would then replicate the storytelling with their own men. As Katie said:

'The campfire was practical, the stories designed to embolden and harden resolve. The point was to bring his team together to focus their minds on the task in hand and to bond them the night before they had to fight together.'

In the days before their own campaign, our modern warriors would do the same.

What I found significant in this, and also a little surprising, was that the Us story was not about 'superhero' ancestors. We have been tricked by films such as *Braveheart* on that. The Us story of those ancient warriors was, rather, focused on practical traits – qualities everyone around the fire could replicate the next day in battle.

The Us story was carefully curated to drive a shared mindset of how to compete in a co-ordinated way. In fact, we learned that the crazed warrior often depicted in films was scorned upon at the time, and it was those who kept composed and stuck to the collective tactics who were most respected and honoured afterwards.

When we shared all of this with the team it shone a new light on how their own culture could be strengthened.

It is this practical application, rather than just a feelgood factor, that underpins the many studies establishing the strong correlation between a team's sense of identity and winning.[32]

During the three-year period of Vern Cotter's tenure as coach of the Scotland team they improved from a world ranking of tenth to fifth.

The outstanding Scotland captain of that era was Greig Laidlaw. Greig grew up a few miles from Melrose Abbey, where the heart of Robert the Bruce is buried. The team became a point of intersection between the players' personal stories and the nation's Us story. Greig recalled:

'Connecting with our identity story was a massive turning point for the team. Before that we were lost. We didn't know who we were or what we were really about. The power of an identity story is that it builds a collective mindset. For us, it was a warrior spirit, that we were ferocious, that we create chaos in others, that we get the job done. This was something we collectively believed in and we played that way.'

Greig highlights here a critical point about an Us story: to have authenticity and true meaning it has to be lived in day-to-day behaviours. Even though fans didn't know the team's inner Us story, they could see those identity traits by the way they played.

When we shared Katie's work with the team, it was as though these ancient warriors of Robert the Bruce's time, known as the 'Flowers of Scotland', had come back to pin the thistles they had worn in battle onto the shirts of the warriors of today.

2.4 extracting our values

OUR STONES

I see values as shorthand for our Us story.

They are the beliefs and traits we value as a tribe. Each of them wrapped in emotive storytelling and passed down our *whakapapa*.

The story of Pakinui was sent to me to explain *this is who we are*. Her story arced with the story of our tribe. Her trauma was our trauma. Her resilience our resilience. Surviving a massacre, starting again, violated, not bowing to disease, evicted from her land again but, returning, prevailing. We look further down our line of people and see these traits in them – we see Paikea, the whale rider, who survived his murderous half-brother.

This storytelling, identifying valued beliefs and traits, shapes a mindset that we have an inherited ability to overcome adversity. That we are resilient people. We start to notice this valued trait in ourselves and those around us. It becomes a standard we aspire to. These values are our super strength.

This shorthand, articulated as values, allows us to align our behaviours. We share a mental map of the world with those around us.

Our values become a code for how we will live and work together. They provide answers to the challenges ahead. This code is less about rules and more about the archetype of the person we aspire to be: a mix of standards (what we are expected to do) and prohibitions (what not to do).

The ancient Polynesian navigators took stones on their double-hulled canoes to represent their tribal values.

I imagine three stones, representing the life force of the tribe, being cleansed in a river to mark them as sacred. They are ceremonially brought on board by the navigator.

Each stone represents a value – a focal point of their Us story.

One stone is blasted from the volcanic bowels of a mountain millennia before. Sent over the land, into the sea, then washed back ashore. This black stone is jagged and scarred. *Resilient*.

A second stone is precious beautiful greenstone (*pounamu*). From a river in another valley, hidden within a dark rock. Unnoticed until split open. Beauty residing in there. Translucent. Smooth. Waiting to unleash itself as a fish hook, a weapon, a treasure. Whatever the moment requires. *Adaptable*.

A third stone comes from the floor of our meeting house in the village. Before that, it came from our home before these islands, where earlier ancestors voyaged from. This stone, with others, formed the foundation of our communal meeting house. A place our culture thrives. A place we are safe. This stone is old. It sacrificed light and warmth for us so we would have a place of belonging. *Selfless*.

These stones are shorthand for our Us story.

TODAY

The power of tribal values has not diminished in our evolutionary story.

One of the iconic publications on corporate teams, *Senior Leadership Teams: What it Takes to Make Them Great*, by Harvard professors (the late) Richard Hackman and Ruth Wageman, shared:

> *Of all the factors that we assessed in our research, the one that makes the biggest difference in how well a senior leadership team performs is the clarity of the behavioural norms that guide members' interaction.*[33]

However, that finding is set against research that only one in four employees either have a strong belief in their organisation's values or apply them in their daily work. [34]

A muscle that seems to have weakened over time is our ancestors' skill in extracting our values from our Us story.

Instead, it is common for values to be disconnected from an organisation's Us story. They stand alone, lacking meaning or narrative. Googled and made into wallpaper. Alternatively, they may be whiteboarded out of thin air. In either case they will likely come out of a bucket of generic values disconnected from authentic identity.

However, people have a sensitive antenna for this. We know when our beliefs have substance and meaning, and we know when we are faking it. We understand that these conversations say much about the strength of our tribal identity.

The need for authenticity in capturing our Us story, and in turn our values, was strikingly captured in a 2008 study undertaken in Manhattan, New York.[35]

The study involved three 'tribes'. One, wealthy upper-middle-class families. Another, relatively stable blue-collar working-class families. The final tribe, poor families surrounded by crime, addiction and homelessness.

The study showed how the values of those 'tribes' mirrored their respective Us stories.

For the 'poor tribe' their stories and values reflected standing your ground and not losing what you had. These values were defensive in nature.

For the 'working-class tribe', their stories and values were about working hard, getting ahead and progressing. These values were aspirational in nature.

In both the poor and working-class tribes there existed a collectivist outlook, respect for power and an authoritarian style of leadership.

For the 'wealthy tribe', who had safety, good health and high living standards, the focus of their stories and values were more individualistic in nature – ideas of personal growth and thriving.

All of these tribes lived in the same geographical area. However, their values and behavioural expectations were fundamentally different as a result of their particular Us story and context.

As Science writer David Berreby puts it, *The engineering of experience is what we call culture.*[36]

We look for proof of our values from our leaders.

We do not want our leaders' personal beliefs forced upon us – we want our tribe's authentic values articulated.

We do not want rules. We want values to aspire to that define what it means to be part of our tribe.

These different models for influencing behaviour were publicly on display at the 2011 Rugby World Cup. Both New Zealand and England had players breach behavioural standards during the tournament.

The All Blacks' approach to dealing with this was for the two players concerned to meet with senior players and explain their behaviour. They were then directed to address the team and apologise. The team itself decided an appropriate sanction. The matter was resolved internally in twenty-four hours without formal processes. The most severe punishment was the shaming that ensued for not meeting the team's archetype of what it was to be an All Black.

In contrast, the three England players concerned were charged with a breach of the rules and summoned to a disciplinary hearing in London weeks later. After a formal hearing the players were found 'guilty' by a judge figure and punished. They were mobbed by the media as they left the hearing.

Two different ways of regulating behaviour: one through values, the other through rules.

ALIGNED

Individuals also carry with them their own personal values.

We address this by standing together in a circle. We look at each other and see the diversity of backgrounds, experiences and identity around us. We are looking at our strength. We respect the journeys and beliefs others carry with them.

We then look to the centre of the circle. Three stones lie there. Each stone represents a core value of this tribe. The leader picks each up in turn and gives it meaning through Us stories: from the past, present and future. The leader hands each stone to a team member. They feel it and hold it. They commune with it. They explain what that value means to them. Then they pass it to the person next to them. In this way, each stone, each value, comes to life.

The leader explains that in this tribe what binds us is a shared identity through our Us story and the values extracted from that.

The leader explains that when we are in this circle our belonging is tied to a tribal way which is sacred to us.

2.5 self . . . less

In 2013, England rugby head coach Stuart Lancaster asked me to help him reconnect the team to its Us story.

In October that year, Stuart gathered the team, along with invited former players, in a small Italian restaurant near his home in Leeds. Stuart and I told the stories.

One of the threads connecting the stories told that evening was the value of *selflessness*.

One story was about Ronnie Poulton, the captain of the England rugby team at the outbreak of the First World War. Ronnie was the supreme attacking player of his generation. He was a star of the 1913 and 1914 undefeated England 'grand slam' winning teams. He captained the team in 1914.

At the outbreak of war, Ronnie (as a part-time territorial soldier) was assigned to home duties within England. However, as England rugby captain he insisted that he should fight on the Western Front. On the morning of 5 May 1915, Ronnie was shot in the trenches at Ploegsteert Wood and killed instantly.

As Ronnie's wooden coffin was pulled by horses down the line, a mass of soldiers lined up to pay their respects. At Waterloo station when the newspaper posters were put up announcing his death there were rarely seen public displays of weeping. Ronnie Poulton was one of twenty-seven former England international rugby players killed in that war.

Moving as this was, it was told as background. The focus of the story that we told took place back on 4 January 1913. This was the day before England's test match against South Africa at Twickenham, London. The narrative told by the newspapers and ensuing history books was that this was one of Ronnie's finest matches for England. He scored a sensational try after a mesmerising forty-yard run and another individual effort from fifty yards out. That was the reported story.

The untold story had been kept within his family. That, unlike the rest of the team, Ronnie had not met up at the hotel the day before the match to prepare. Instead, he'd sent a telegram to the team's management advising that he would be staying in Oxford that evening and would catch a train on the morning of the match. Why?

As a student at Oxford University Ronnie and some friends had established a boys' club in the city that would meet on a weekday evening. Working-class boys would come and meet heroes like Ronnie, play games with them and chat. After leaving university and joining the family's business (the Palmer biscuit factory) Ronnie had continued the boys' club despite his various other commitments.

During the winter of 1913 one of the boys in the club had developed a serious illness. On Ronnie's way to the train station to travel down to London for the match, a man came up to him and said, 'Mr Poulton, I just want to wish you the very best for the match. I also wanted you to know that Johnny is very unwell. He's in the infirmary and isn't expected to be with us much longer. I just wanted to thank you for everything you have given him and done for him.'

Ronnie spoke with the boy's father and insisted that he go

back to the infirmary to see the dying boy. Ronnie, along with the boy's parents, stayed at his bedside through the night until the boy passed away.

Ronnie then went home for a few hours before catching the early train to London. One can only imagine how emotionally and physically spent Ronnie was that day he played his greatest game. Outside of his family, Ronnie never spoke of the reason for his delayed meeting up with the team.

Selfless.

2.6 identity vacuum

We look to our leaders to be the storyteller-in-chief and expect them to personify our tribal identity.

We do not want our Us story replaced by a leader's Me story, a cult of personality, with the rest of us as supporting cast.

Neither do we exist to merely execute plans or strategies or KPI's disconnected from an Us story. That is soulless.

Studies show how storytelling ability enhances a leader's influence and power through shifting the hormonal state of the group.[37]

Our ancestors understood this. Ideas like *whakapapa* people-proof tribal identity, ensuring that the transmission of culture down the line of people is not perverted by the agenda of individuals.

Many organisations create a vacuum around their Us story by asking external agencies to define it for them before they have deeply captured it themselves. What comes back is often a story and message that it's perceived the public want to hear, rather than the authentic story.

When our Us story is weak, we are weak.

Our primal need for an identity story means that when it is untold by our leaders then that vacuum will be filled by another version. There is always a storyline attached to what we are doing in teams.

A self-constructed Us story will come from our subjective experiences and what those around us say. It may be shaped by gossip and highly weighted to recent events. Whether slanted positively or negatively, a series of self-constructed Us stories does not build collective cohesion. The versions of these stories may vary wildly depending where on the status spectrum you sit.

This lack of a shared Us story is a recipe for misalignment and a weak sense of togetherness.

For high-profile teams, conventional media and social media have their own version of a team's Us story and relentlessly communicate it. Those versions are an outside impression. They can be more cartoon than narrative, often distorted by a few dramatic incidents. Despite this, through repetition, they can become 'accepted wisdom' and be adopted by team members themselves.

This external version of Us becomes our version of Us. The strengths and weaknesses the outside world sees in us, we come to see in ourselves. The likely outcomes they see for us, we foresee. We play for their external approval so we can stay in the story they are telling. Our motivation shifts to pleasing this external teller of the story.

A classic example is England football's so-called 'Golden Generation' team that played between 2001 and 2010. The team included world-class players such as David Beckham, Paul Scholes, Steven Gerrard, Frank Lampard, Rio Ferdinand and Michael Owen. This 'Golden Generation' team was mired by inconsistency and failed to live up to expectations in major tournaments. They became a byword for unfulfilled potential.

One of the world's leading football coaches, Pep Guardiola, has stated that the 'Golden Generation' team had comparable talent with the Spanish team that over the same period won a World Cup and European Championship.[38] The 'Golden Generation' team never got beyond the quarter-final of either.

Between 1998 and 2008 Michael Owen was a fully paid up member of the 'Golden Generation' team, playing eighty-nine matches for England and scoring forty goals. He played in three World Cups and two European Championships. Reflecting on his England career, Michael shared with me:

'The media shaped how we saw ourselves. There was no other version provided within the team. Players were scared of making mistakes and being vilified by the media. The performances became more about quietening the media rather than a sense of our own story.'

This dynamic was fed by the lack of an Us story within the England football team. Michael continues:

'Over the whole of my England career, within the dressing room there was never any mention of the team's history, nor what it was to be English.'

Instead, the narrative was heavily weighted to the tactical and technical. It was about the *how* without the *what* and *why*.

Michael recalls Sven-Göran Eriksson, when he was England manager, seeking to transform the team's play from the traditional British style to a more continental possession-based game. However, there was a serious problem. The carriers of the England football team's Us story, the media, did not understand or approve of this new style of play. Their version of England's Us story involved a traditional game comprising speed, high energy and physicality. This identity clash held the team back on the field as Michael explains:

'The media and crowds had this bulldog identity – they wanted to see the players chasing everything, being physical, playing at a hundred miles an hour and showing passion. But that was not the way successful international teams played. When we tried to slow the play down, we would be criticised for a lack of passion and showing no fight. The manager was accused of the same thing. Some players found it easier to give in and play in the traditional way so they wouldn't be criticised. We never fully played the style of football that we could have.'

These are rich insights in understanding why that 'Golden Generation' team never achieved its full potential.

Michael contrasts his England experiences with his time at Manchester United under Sir Alex Ferguson, for whom he played three seasons. There was no identity vacuum there. Michael recalls, when being recruited by Manchester United, that Sir Alex invited him to his house. In that initial chat between them Sir Alex took Michael through the club's powerful identity story and what it meant to wear that red shirt.

Michael recalls how, before a crucial Champions League fixture, Sir Alex held a team meeting three hours ahead of kick-off. The players assumed they were in for a tactical reminder. Instead, Sir Alex, in a calm conversational tone, retraced the essence of the club's Us story, spoke about his and their own journeys and how these had led to this opportunity to create another piece of history for the club. Michael recalls:

'I was not someone for motivational talks. I liked to prepare calmly on my own. But this was different. That was the best team talk I ever heard. It was calm, there was no shouting. It was about being selfless and leaving a legacy.'

In 2016 I was engaged by the English Football Association to help capture their Us story and cascade it into the various national teams.

The simpler the approach to the Us story, the more impact it seems to have. I started on this project by looking at the national shirt and the three lions symbol. Where did the lion symbol come from? What does it represent?

I arranged a visit to the National Archives in Kew Gardens, London. There, a gloved expert on English monarchs brought out to me the first seal of the three lions. It was from 1197 when King Richard I (Richard the Lionheart) had made the Anjou family coat of arms the emblem for England. I was able to hold the seal that King Richard had used over eight hundred years before. This was where the three lions symbol came from. A sacred artefact from the team's *whakapapa*.

I was told how the lions represented both leading and taking care of others, as well as fearlessness and ferocity. What also quickly emerged was that the lion is, of course, not just a traditional British symbol but has equal power across Africa and Asia. This idea resonated strongly with the diverse nature of English society today, and the individuals that represent their nation in sport.

The genesis story of the three lions symbol, and its original meaning, flowed directly into the Us story that we worked on and then shared with the players.

England team head coach Gareth Southgate has his own deep connection to the three lions. A former England international himself, involved in a dramatic penalty shoot-out loss to Germany in the 1996 Euros semi-final, Gareth had by now found the future more compelling than ruminating on the past. Over time he had developed a vision for the next part of the team's Us story. He was determined that at the 2018 FIFA World Cup in Russia his team would write its own inspiring chapter.

Despite being the least experienced team at the tournament, and the youngest England team to ever appear at a World Cup, the team exceeded external expectations and their world ranking, ultimately losing in extra time in their semi-final against Croatia.

Gareth sought to free the team from external pressures by focusing on what they could control. This was neither the past nor a negative external Us story. This focus on controlling their own destiny empowered the team. After England defeated Columbia in a last sixteen knockout match, their first ever penalty shoot-out win at a World Cup, Gareth described that milestone in this way:

'We've spoken to the players about writing their own stories. Tonight they showed they don't have to conform to what's gone before. They have created their own. It'll hopefully give belief to the generations of players that will follow.'[39]

As Gareth says, writing their own chapter of the Us story 'did not mean loose talk of winning the tournament but rather targeting plotlines along the way': moving out of their group, winning a knockout game, winning their first ever World Cup penalty shoot-out; reconnecting with the nation; expressing themselves without fear; having an adventure together; creating lifelong bonds with each other.

The team's identity on and off the field was built around three values that reflect a contemporary inclusive sense of what it is to be English. For the time being, those values remain sacred within the dressing room.

After the World Cup we asked some respected international football coaches to describe the England team they saw in that tournament. It was reaffirming that they typically used either the exact words of our values or close synonyms. This was evidence of a growing authentic identity.

In this way, through renewing their values and consciously writing their own chapter, the team filled a vacuum and quietened the noise of external scriptwriters.

2.7 building an inclusive 'Us' story

Kotahi te kohao o te ngira e kuhuna ai te miro ma, te miro pango me te miro whero.

(There is but one single eye of the needle through which the white, black and red threads must pass.)

Māori proverb

I have always found the Olympic Games a particularly emotional experience. Tears were never far away when our small nation would win a medal, watch our flag unfurled and have our national anthem played before the world.

I recall as a seven-year-old our headmaster bringing the whole school together in the library to watch our own John Walker win the 1,500m gold medal at the 1976 Montreal Olympics.

One afternoon during holidays a decade later the Olympic games would come to take on an even deeper meaning for me.

As part of excavating my own identity story I drove out to my uncle Jim Daly's farm under the Takitimu Mountains. The coastal boundary of his farm was lined by Monterey cypress trees bent by wild southerly winds. Like Jim himself, their roots were deep and refused to yield. As far as you could see, the crook of the coast marched belligerently up the island.

Jim was a humorous genial old man by then, having retired

from his working life as a sheep farmer. I wanted to talk with him about his experiences in the Second World War.

I knew Jim had fought with the New Zealand division of the Allied Forces in North Africa, including at the famous battle of El Alamein, and then later in Italy, where he took part in the Battle of Monte Cassino. However, nobody in my family seemed to know any of the detail. So, I decided to ask him. Jim was very forthcoming and happy to answer my questions.

It was a memorable afternoon in a number of ways. There was a lesson in it about how many layers sit below the exterior we present to the world. It also highlighted the fragility of our Us stories and how this part of my *whakapapa*, from my mother's side this time, could so easily have been lost.

On my way home that day the story that most dominated my thoughts, and still does decades later, related to Jim's experience in the Allied defeat of the German forces in the Battle of El Alamein, a town on Egypt's Mediterranean coast.

Jim told me that the New Zealand forces, with the Māori Battalion at the forefront, led the Allies' night-time attack. Jim explained that at one point during the chaos he and his mate became dislocated from their unit and, with shells exploding around them, jumped into a hole. However, two German soldiers also seeking shelter were already in it.

A fight ensued and it was settled that the Kiwi soldiers would take the Germans as prisoners. One of the German soldiers had been a student at Cambridge University in England at the outbreak of the war and had been forced to join the German army though he despised the Nazis. Jim said the Germans were good people. The four men shared their provisions during the evening, remaining in their sanctuary until dawn.

Next morning, without any sleep, and with the Germans as prisoners, Jim reconnected with his unit.

Exhausted, Jim asked his sergeant major if he could have a short sleep but was told that was not going to happen as there were German bodies around that needed to be buried. So, Jim and three other soldiers went about this laborious and grisly task.

Jim became uncharacteristically emotional when he recalled burying one particular German soldier. After the grave was dug, Jim was at the top lifting the soldier's shoulders as they lowered him in. Jim suddenly felt something hard under the German's shirt and told the others to stop. They put this soldier down on the side of his grave so they could check what this hard object was.

Upon unbuttoning the shirt Jim found a gold medal from the 1936 Berlin Olympics around the dead man's neck. Jim explained how, for the first time that awful morning, all the men just stared at the soldier's face, the inhumanity of what they were doing dawning on them. Jim said he wept at the side of that grave.

The poignancy of Jim's memory was the first thing I thought of in 2018 when I was approached to work with the British Olympic team, known as Team GB, as it prepared for the Tokyo Olympics.

Team GB, in partnership with the athletes themselves, had been on a journey to develop and deepen their Us story from before the 2012 London Olympics.

What made this work particularly compelling was the sheer diversity of Team GB: gender, race, religion, ethnicity, colour, sexuality, family status, not to mention personality, the part of Great Britain they come from and the fact the team itself is made up of thirty-three different sports. The team is a mirror of the British nation unlike any other.

The BOA had realised that just wearing the uniform was not enough to instil a genuine sense of belonging in athletes and staff. There needed to be an inclusive Us story that each of this diverse group of individuals could attach personal meaning to.

From a performance perspective, this sense of belonging, of feeling they fitted in and mattered, would be a key step in enabling athletes to access their talent on the biggest stage.

Team GB's Chef de Mission Mark England had personalised this challenge:

'I had an insight into how important this was with Team GB at the 2015 European Games in Baku. One of our athletes was a world and commonwealth champion but she was eliminated early at those games. I could sense that she was not right in Baku, uncomfortable, withdrawn. I made time to check in on her. She said she had been homesick, that she didn't feel she fitted into the team environment. From that moment, I made it a personal mission to make sure that nobody else would feel that way and be held back from delivering their best.'

What was required was an Us story each individual could connect with. As a friend of mine once told me, 'Put up a Christmas tree and allow each individual to decorate it in their own personal way.'

The approach we took was to use the team's diversity as a lens to look at its incredible heritage and special place in the hearts of the British people.

We used Team GB's *whakapapa* to shine a light on inspiring forebears who would connect across the diversity of the team.

From this work, some powerful pioneering figures stepped out of the shadows.

We brought back into the light Charlotte Cooper who in 1900 became the first British female to compete in an Olympic Games and also the first to medal, winning gold in the women's singles and the mixed doubles' tennis.

We remembered the fifty-one members of Team GB who were killed in the First World War and the sixteen in the Second World War. One of those First World War causalities was Noel Chavasse, who was killed in the Battle of Passchendaele in 1917. He was a doctor who became a captain in the Royal Army Medical Corps and won the Victoria Cross twice for his courage recovering wounded soldiers from the battlefield (the only soldier in that war to win the Victoria Cross twice).[40] Noel had represented Team GB in the 400m at the 1908 London Olympics.

Harry Edward was introduced to today's generation. Harry was the first black athlete to represent Team GB in an Olympic Games, winning bronze medals in the 100m and 200m in Antwerp in 1920 (the games preceding the famed *Chariots of Fire* film). Harry had been born in Berlin to a German mother and Guyanese father. He had been interred in a camp in Germany during the First World War before relocating to London after the war ended. For many years the media had incorrectly reported Jack London, 100m medallist in Stockholm 1928, as Team GB's first black athlete.

Moving along the line of forebears, the light was paused on the 1972 Women's sprinting team who competed in the Munich Games. This lightning combination heralded the emergence of female black athletes in Team GB with Andrea Lynch, Sonia

Lannaman and Anita Neil, who had become Team GB's first female black athlete in the 1968 Mexico City Games.

With Team GB in the 1984 Los Angeles Games, we celebrated men's hockey player Kulbir Bhaura, who became the first Sikh Team GB athlete, and rower Salih Hassan, who became the first Muslim to medal.

The team's diversity around sexuality was highlighted through recent champions such as Tom Daley in diving, Nicola Adams in boxing and the married couple Kate and Helen Richardson-Walsh in women's hockey.

Out of this long Us story, Team GB's four values (unity, respect, responsibility, pride) have taken on new meaning as shorthand for the story.

Mark England reflected with me on the ongoing excavation of Team GB's Us story in this way:

'As the stories from the past emerged, they have added a richness to individuals' sense of belonging. Everyone could see that they had a place in this team, it was a safe place and they were welcome. That they could just focus on their performances. That they were part of an unbroken chain of people that each left a legacy.'

This sense of 'legacy' that Mark refers to was deepened by sharing the deeds of Team GB in 1964 – the last time they competed in Tokyo. In reconnecting to that inspirational team, I spent time with key members such as Ann Packer, who won Team GB's first ever female track gold medal in the 800m, and her husband, Robbie Brightwell, the athletics team captain and winner himself of a silver medal in the 400m.

A significant legacy of that 1964 team was to forever transform women's sport in Great Britain. This started with gold medal swimmer Anita Lonsbrough becoming the first ever female flag bearer from any nation in the Summer Games. It was bolstered by Team GB's first two track and field female gold medallists: Mary Rand in the long jump and then Ann Packer. Both attractive, self-confident, humble, articulate and very relatable to the public, Mary and Ann projected a new image of women's sport. Both had normal jobs (Mary in the post office and Ann as a teacher) and Mary had a daughter, Alison. Many regard these two women as popularising women's sport at the time and believe that this catalysed the remarkable success of female Team GB athletes in subsequent generations. When the team returns to Tokyo in 2021 it will, for the first time, most likely include more female athletes than male.

It has been important to understand the legacy of the 1964 team, the chapter that team wrote. This motivates the current Team GB to go and write its own history in a time when the country is looking to be inspired and feel united.

We have come to see Tokyo as a sacred place where, in a sense, our ancestors are waiting for us.

Team GB's inclusive Us story keeps revealing itself before our eyes.

In early 2020 Georgina Harland was named as Team GB's first ever female Chef de Mission for the Olympic Winter Games to be held in Beijing in 2022.

The sun has revealed Georgie as another female pioneer in Team GB's *whakapapa* to join the likes of Charlotte Cooper, Anita Lonsbrough and Anita Neil, as well as skater Mollie Phillips who in the 1936 Winter Games in Bavaria, Germany, became the first female flag bearer of any nation. Reflecting on her appointment, Georgie told me:

> 'Team GB has inspired the direction of my life since the age of eight and so I am extremely proud to have the opportunity to add another thread to the already rich identity story of this team. If this next chapter can provide the catalyst for any athlete or staff member to connect with Team GB, in a way they otherwise wouldn't have, that would be incredible.'

2.8 carving the pain into our walls

When we deny the story, it defines us. When we own the story, we can create a brave new ending.

Brené Brown

A few years ago, in the midst of a public controversy around a team I had worked with, I spoke with one of its cultural architects: a Māori spiritual adviser. I asked his view on how resilient the culture would be to what was an act of stupidity that had led to shame and significant financial and reputational fallout. He replied, 'The culture will be strong but we must carve this story into our walls. How else will our descendants learn from our experiences?'

In the words of Oxford University's Chair of Social Anthropology, Harvey Whitehouse, the sharing of painful experiences can produce 'identity fusion'.[41] Whitehouse and his team have identified two key performance benefits that can come from such pain: more intense togetherness and critical practical lessons. American social psychologist Naomi Eisenberger puts it like this:

> ... *the experience of social pain, although distressing and hurtful in the short-term, is an evolutionary adaptation that promotes social bonding and ultimately survival.*[42]

I found a powerful example of this in my work with the English FA. A moment that caused pain, suffering and indignity in women's football in England that persists to this day.

Here you find strong figures in the game today continue to reference a dark event that took place nearly one hundred years ago.

On 5 December 1921 the English FA passed a resolution banning its member clubs from allowing women to play on their grounds and for any FA-affiliated person to be involved in the women's game. Concerns over compatibility of football with female health were cited as official reasons:

The council feel impelled to express their strong opinion that the game of football is quite unsuitable for females and ought not to be encouraged. The council requests the clubs belonging to the association refuse the use of their club grounds for such matches.

That 'ban' remained in place for fifty years. And it was not until 1993, a further twenty-two years later, that the FA brought women's football within its own structure.

The background to the FA's resolution was that during the First World War, when the professional men's leagues were suspended, women's football in England had become a box office hit. Women's matches raised millions for wounded soldiers' charities and match attendance skyrocketed.

The high-water mark of women's football during this period was Boxing Day 1920. Dick, Kerr Ladies played St Helens Ladies in front of fifty-five thousand people at Goodison Park in Liverpool (with an estimated further fourteen thousand outside unable to gain entry). It has been said that this one match raised today's equivalent of £600,000 for charity.

In 1921 Dick, Kerr Ladies had nine hundred thousand people watch them over the course of sixty-seven matches. They were attracting larger attendances than most professional men's games. By the end of that year they were banned.

Many hold the view that commercial reasons influenced the FA's decision: concerns that the large crowds to women's games were suppressing spectator numbers in the professional men's games.

Effectively overnight, the FA ban resulted in women superstars of the time, such as Lily Parr, going from playing in front of tens of thousands of people, and having merchandise produced using their image, to playing in front of a handful of people in a public park. Lily herself became a mental health nurse working with soldiers suffering from post-traumatic stress.

From playing in front of thousands and being written about in the newspapers, the elite women players became anonymous. From using first-class facilities they now changed in cars and sheds. From playing on the best pitches in the land, they paid to use muddy bogs used after the men's games had finished over the weekend. From all of their expenses covered they now had to pay subs, pay for their kit, pay for pitch hire and pile into cars to keep petrol costs down.

England football superstar of the time Tom Finney said:

'I remember being invited to referee several of their [Dick, Kerr Ladies] matches and being presented to the girls. There wasn't much women's football in those days and to actually see them play was quite remarkable. Some of them were very good players and they always had big crowds. I knew the FA did not look very kindly upon them and it was thought we professional players should not encourage them.[43]

During those decades in the darkness, women's football did manage to survive in England. Despite the obstruction and indignities, a genuine love for the game prevailed. But they never forgot how they had been treated. Neither did they forget the resilience of their ancestors who kept the game alive, a game that is now flourishing and is full of professional opportunities for talented women players.

This ban by the FA still generates significant pain and a sense of loss as to 'what could have been' over those years.

I spoke with Hope Powell about this. Hope is a force of nature. She was an England women's international and later became the first full-time national coach of the team (the Lionesses) between 1998 and 2013. By being appointed to this role, Hope became the first black national coach in England and the first LGBT national coach in English sport.

As a player, Hope had been the first black player to represent the England women's team, along with Brenda Sempare, in a match against the Republic of Ireland on 9 September 1983.

Much of the Lionesses' recent success can be directly traced to the elite level and grass roots initiatives Hope was involved in introducing.

When reflecting on the FA's 1921 resolution, Hope calls it 'disgusting' and 'shameful'. Beyond those feelings, Hope says she is stuck with the question 'what if . . . ?' What if this ban had never happened? What would the women's game look like today? It's a great question. Hope makes a compelling point that if an alien had visited Liverpool on Boxing Day 1920 and found a sell-out crowd of fifty-five thousand spectators at Goodison Park for a women's game, then seen some top men's games attracting a fraction of that, they would have concluded that the dominant game was the women's game.

Hope reflects on her tenure as head coach of the England women's team and being labelled by some as 'difficult' and 'pushy'. The lesson she took from the pain of the 1921 resolution and adopted in her work was that if you didn't stand up for yourself and fight for what you believed in, then what you treasured could be taken away. She saw the experience of her parents who migrated from the Caribbean in the 1960s as mirroring this lesson.

Many in the women's game fear that with the professionalism and increased equality of modern elite women's football, players could become disconnected from this part of their Us story. To the FA's credit, notwithstanding its own historic role in the story, it too keeps the facts and fallout of the 1921 resolution alive in its role as custodians of the women's game.

The message is clear: strong cultures don't airbrush history.

Why would we turn a blind eye to such valuable lessons within our Us story? That would be self-destructive, yet how often do we see it today after perceived failures? An oversimplified explanation is produced, often a single 'cause'. A human sacrifice is made. A new hero, often from another tribe and with a different Us story, replaces the old one who has become associated with the pain. The unpalatable past is erased from conversation, left unresolved, too uncomfortable to recall. We start again with a clean whiteboard. The new hero writes their wisdom, from another place and context, on it.

Our ancestors would regard this reflex as madness. They understood that we only get better by learning from past experiences, both good and bad. That progress is an iterative process, with experiences and lessons layered upon each other. That changing leaders is the last, not the first, measure to consider.

That an even worse outcome than coming back to the village without food is not to understand why.

3

feeding the village

Look at every path closely. Then ask yourself, and yourself alone, the question: does this path have a heart?
Carlos Castenada, *The Teachings of Don Juan*

3.1 serving others

A few months after Michael Campbell's 2005 US Golf Open victory he went on to win the World Matchplay Championship at Wentworth in England. Michael has not won another golf tournament since. Commentators and fans have speculated that Michael lost motivation and focus after these career-defining and financially lucrative wins. There is truth in that, though not in the way they think.

To understand Michael's story, you need to go back twenty-five years. Michael, then aged twelve, was staying on his maternal grandparents' farm over a weekend. It was a family gathering: grandparents, uncles, aunties and around fifty cousins, all spending time together on the farm.

In the midst of the fun and chaos, Michael's grandmother asked him to take a walk with her across a field. Just the two of them.

Michael had a special relationship with his grandmother, and they would often stay up late into the night chatting. She practised traditional Māori medicine and was regarded as a spiritual healer. Once, when Michael had glandular fever, his grandmother used special water from the farm to cure it. Michael recovered quickly without needing to see a medical practitioner. The connection between them stayed strong, even after she passed away when Michael was sixteen.

On this afternoon, as the two of them walked across the field, Michael's grandmother told him that he needed to prepare himself because he was going to achieve something very special in his life which would bring *mana* to others: his family, his tribe, the Māori people and New Zealand.

Mana is not only a Māori concept but a wider Polynesian spiritual idea. It is sometimes translated as 'respect' but that is inadequate. Beyond respect, it is a spiritual expression of esteem that others give to a person or group. This is important – you cannot define or decide your own *mana*, it can only be bestowed by others. The regard in which a person is held is influenced by their own deeds and that of the groups they belong to.

Mana is never fixed; it can advance or retreat depending on you or your group's actions. The greater those deeds, and crucially your selflessness and humility in the way you carry yourself, the more *mana* is bestowed.

Similarly, if our own *mana* is enhanced, then so is that of our family and team and tribe; if our own *mana* is diminished by our actions, then so is that of the groups we belong to. If others in our group act in a way that changes the group's *mana*, then this also reflects on us personally. Our status and esteem are tied to our belonging – we are interdependent.

Mana is a powerful idea, gifted to us by our ancestors, that makes us indivisible from the groups we belong to. We prosper or suffer together. It is a practical and powerful means of aligning behaviour and strengthening the bond of a group.

As they walked together on the farm, Michael's grandmother emphasised to him his need to work hard and stay humble, so he would be ready for his fate. That a path would open for him to achieve something special for his people. There was no mention of what sphere of life this achievement would be in; Michael was not even pursuing golf at this age.

This was Michael's purpose that he fulfilled in the summer of 2005. In doing so he brought *mana* to others through his golfing success and the humble way he carried himself. He made others think more highly of his family, his tribe, the Māori people and New Zealand as a nation.

To me, this explains the arc of Michael's career. Replicating his success of that year would have been satisfying, of course, and profitable, but could never exceed the impact Michael had already achieved by delivering on the collective purpose that drove him.

3.2 our why

The first warrior looked out on the land that was his home. He saw the hills and the stars and he was happy. For giving him his home, the first warrior told the Great Spirit that he would fight and win many battles in his honor. But the Great Spirit said, "No, do not fight for me. Fight for your tribe, fight for the family born to you, fight for the brothers you find. Fight for them," the Great Spirit said, "for they are your home."[44]

Oglala Lakota Chief Henry Standing Bear

Michael Campbell's story provides an important insight into human motivation, one borne out by our evolutionary story.

Our most powerful form of motivation is a collective, rather than personal, cause. A cause fuelled by our sense of belonging.

Iconic organisational psychologist Edgar Schein puts it plainly:

'The word and concept of 'purpose' comes out of psychology. I have learned that most of what comes out of psychology is kind of useless in this human arena. I'm a psychologist, so I'm entitled to say that. But the psychologists have never learned that everything that goes on inside motivation, purpose, and so on is based on a culture, a group, a tribe . . .'[45]

The idea of individual purpose is relatively recent in the *homo sapien*'s story. It seems to track alongside the introduction of agriculture around ten thousand years ago. This was the stage in our evolutionary story when villages became towns and towns became cities. Personal property took hold and reliance on small bands of kin receded.

Over the past two and a half thousand years democracy, individual liberty, free enterprise and consumerism have emerged and been widely adopted. This shift to individualism was accelerated by the 'Age of Enlightenment' three hundred years ago.

Individualistic societies prevail in the Western world and dominate popular culture but there are many traditionally collectivist societies in the world where the question 'what is your personal purpose in life?' is met with a blank stare.

In high-performing environments, I've seen questions of 'personal purpose' put to athletes and often what comes back is either a similar blank stare or something quickly invented to make the question go away. The modern level of focus, and often anguish, involved in defining personal purpose or mission in life has never made much sense to me. It is not a question that was considered by my ancestors, including my parents.

I put this question to All Black Jerome Kaino in our conversation for this book and his reply reflects how I feel myself: 'I cannot say I have a personal purpose or mission, it is one hundred per cent about what my family and teams need from me.'

For sure, some individuals have a burning personal source of motivation and ambition, sometimes fuelled by specific circumstances in their background. However, we should not feel inadequate if we don't have clarity of purpose at an individualistic level.

To have a personal cause outside the group's purpose would have historically risked shaming, punishment and exclusion. We hunted, we gathered, we foraged, we cared for others, we raised children with and for each other. Our wellbeing was inextricably tied to the tribe's success. In this way, our evolutionary story built a motivational framework that was interwoven with the tribe's interests.

To survive required us to compete and this too became hard-wired in our biology and psychology. We can only survive by competing – with our environment, with other species, with the climate, with Them. Competing was what we did together. The Latin origin of the word 'compete' involves 'striving together'.

Today, despite our shared evolutionary story, individuals can come into teams with very different motivational models depending on whether they were conditioned by a more traditional collectivist society or a more individualistic one. Professor Robert Sapolsky puts it this way:

Your life will be unrecognisably different depending on what culture the stork deposited you into.[46]

In his book *Behave*, Sapolsky sets out the fundamental differences between 'collectivist' and 'individualist' societies around the world today.

In collectivist societies behaviour is dominated by the needs of the group. The focus for people is their relationships with others. This, in turn, drives high levels of conformity and harmony. Conflict, shame and standing out are actively averted in these cultures. Competitiveness is more about status and not falling behind, rather than dominating others.

Many cultures around the world retain a sense of purpose and identity that can only be understood in relation to their family, tribe and church. This feeds into how they approach being part of teams. This is the world of Michael Campbell and Jerome Kaino. It remains pervasive in Africa and Asia and Polynesia.

Sapolsky describes individualist societies, such as the United States, United Kingdom and other Western capitalist democracies, as having veered off in another direction. In these societies, the needs and rights of individuals prevail; an ethos of 'looking out for number one'.[47]

A creeping shift has taken place from what is 'our' purpose to what is 'my' purpose. Sapolsky identifies autonomy, personal achievement and a sense of our own unique identity as underpinning social norms in individualist societies:

Motivation and satisfaction are gained from self- rather than group-derived effort. Competitive drive is about getting ahead of everyone else.[48]

These individualistic values actually work against our need to belong. They push a mindset of seeing ourselves against rather than with others.

When asked to draw a diagram of their social network Americans tend to put their own circle in the centre of the page and make it the largest. However, East Asian collectivist cultures draw their circle far from the centre and considerably smaller.[49]

This individualist view of the world has been exacerbated by the internet. It has reduced our perceived reliance on 'elders' or experts. We can google whatever we want to know and choose our own tribes. We can enter or leave those tribes on a whim. All of this heightens our sense of self first and diminishes our sense of belonging.

The primacy of collective over individual purpose is captured in our biology. Performance psychologist Michael Gervais explains how our biology drives this motivation:

As Maslow explains, survival is a base need. Once that is secured, we want to help others. Our body rewards us for selfless action through serotonin, oxytocin, dopamine and endorphins – we don't get those same hits when we are only serving self-interest.

This can be further understood by reflecting on Abraham Maslow's famous 'Hierarchy of Needs' model. In Maslow's model the base need of humans is physiological for survival (such as food, water, warmth). The next level of need is safety. Then our need for belonging. Maslow calls these three levels our basic needs. Once they are met, we move to the psychological need for esteem. The final level of need is self-actualisation.

Whilst self-actualisation may sound very individualistic, contemporary researchers of this work connect this state with serving others. One of the leading researchers in this field, Scott Barry Kaufman, Professor at the University of Pennsylvania's Positive Psychology Center, explains:

It is clear that Maslow never conceptualized self-actualizing people as selfish or purely individualistic ... self-actualized people use their full powers in the service of others.[50]

Performance psychologist David Galbraith, who works with the Japanese national rugby team as well as Olympic champions, shares this observation from inside dressing rooms:

'In those last few minutes before performers go out to compete, personal meaning always returns to family and a deep connection to teammates. This is when the space becomes very quiet, very peaceful, very spiritual. Individual aspirations taper off in those last few moments.'

Good leaders articulate a collective purpose that fires up this motivation. They align everyone to a goal that benefits the collective first and individuals second.

Much is written about *intrinsic* versus *extrinsic* motivation. They can coexist in a healthy way when a team has a strong collective purpose: we are intrinsically motivated to belong to the group and want to contribute towards its success. In achieving this, we receive personal recognition through affirmation, status and rewards.

However, when a meaningful shared purpose is missing then extrinsic motivation often prevails and, with that, self-interested behaviours. This weakens a team. This is not how our species evolved the super strength of powerful teamwork.

Leaders need to be mindful that diverse teams include people who have been conditioned by very different models of the world. However, all are receptive to a well-articulated collective purpose.

So, what is the common ground between these collectivist and individualist models of the world that the stork has randomly deposited us into?

Personal meaning.

Once a common purpose has been articulated, each person should have an opportunity to attach personal meaning to it.

For those from individualist societies, this part of the process is particularly important. They need space to work through how the collective purpose also enhances them personally. For many from collectivist societies, that understanding is innate, and they will spend little time personalising it.

Former All Blacks coach Wayne Smith captures this leadership challenge in his own potent way: 'Creating a champion team is a spiritual challenge.' It is worth breaking this quote down. The definition of spirituality has two limbs. First, an individual connecting to a purpose greater than their own. Second, profound emotional communion between people.

Whakapapa helps the All Blacks capture this. It connects individuals to a higher purpose than their own and establishes deep emotional connection between them. It keeps purpose alive and real with the idea of it being passed down a line of people, each in turn seeking to deliver on that in their time in the sun.

Wayne Smith's words are echoed by the most successful NBA coach of all time, Phil Jackson. The following words come from *Sacred Hoops*, which Jackson wrote in the middle of the Chicago Bulls' run of six championships in the 1990s (which, of course, was led by the ultimate alpha Michael Jordan):

> . . . *working with the Bulls, I've learned that the most effective way to forge a winning team is to call on the players' need to connect with something larger than themselves. Even for those who do not consider themselves 'spiritual' in a conventional sense, creating a successful team . . . is essentially a spiritual act. It requires the individuals involved to surrender their*

*self-interest for the greater good so that the whole adds up to
more than the sum parts.*[51]

This, therefore, is the apex in teams: a powerful shared purpose
where individuals attach deeper personal meaning to that cause.

3.3 *ubuntu*

We belong in a bundle of life. Ubuntu *says: a person
is a person through other persons. It says: I am human
because I belong.*

Archbishop Desmond Tutu

Ubuntu *for us means the measure of our lives is our
impact on others.*

the Proteas

To the ancestral gifts bequeathed to us, we can add *ubuntu* from
our African kin.

Ubuntu comes from the indigenous people of southern Africa,
and became the heart of the transformed team culture of the
South African national cricket team (known as the Proteas after
the national flower they wear on their shirts).

As with all the spiritual ideas shared in this book, *ubuntu* has
a particular source of origin, but is a universal idea shared across
humanity.

This was brought home to me many years after the Hennops
River camp described in the pages that follow. I was reading about
the life of Jackie Robinson, who in 1947 became the first player
to break through the colour barrier in major league baseball. In

110

the story was a photograph of Robinson's tombstone. Other than the great man's name, the only engraved words were *A life is not important except in the impact it has on other lives.*

Ubuntu.

These ancient ideas of collective purpose are part of our shared heritage.

The Proteas' story of coming home to *ubuntu* can only be understood by an appreciation of South Africa's political context in the twentieth century.

Despite growing up two oceans away, South Africa's tortured story was something my own country was deeply intertwined with.

Between 1948 and 1990 South Africa had a formal system of institutionalised racial segregation (known as 'apartheid'). Under this authoritarian political regime access to institutions, housing, employment and geographic areas was determined by racial categories. White citizens had the highest status, followed by Asians and 'Coloureds', then black Africans. It was a system based on white supremacy.

Within my country's own Us story, a sense of shame still sits in our failure to do better in our relationship with South Africa.

In 1928 the All Blacks toured South Africa for the first time. The South African authorities requested that only white players be selected. Our administrators complied. This meant that arguably the best player in the world at the time, the All Blacks Māori full back George Nepia, was excluded from selection, along with other leading players such as Lui Paewai and Jimmy Mill.

The same request and the same compliance occurred again in the All Blacks' tours to South Africa in 1949 and then again in 1960, with the 1960 tour taking place just months after the Sharpeville Massacre where in a township fifty miles south of Johannesburg police officers opened fire on unarmed protesters, killing 69 and wounding 180. George Nepia himself joined the protests on the streets against the 1960 tour. In his memoir he reflected:

> ... we were saddened, disappointed and humiliated by [the New Zealand Rugby Union] which purported to be our guide, philosopher and friend.[52]

In 1970 the All Blacks toured South Africa again. This time, under mounting international pressure, the South African authorities reluctantly permitted ethnic Māori and Samoan players to be on the team provided they were officially labelled as 'honorary whites'. Our administrators accepted this proposal.

In 1976 the All Blacks again toured South Africa, and again, Māori and Samoan players were officially labelled as 'honorary whites'. This tour started exactly two weeks after the Soweto Uprising where hundreds of student protesters were shot dead by police. That tour took place amidst an international boycott of South African sport and resulted in significant condemnation. As a result of this All Blacks tour, twenty-two African nations boycotted the 1976 Olympic Games in Montreal due to the presence of my small country.

These painful events need to be carved into our own walls.

In 1991, after the fall of apartheid, the Proteas became the nation's first multi-cultural representative cricket team. Prior to that time there were various national cricket teams, each representing a racial category. The whites-only team were, like the rugby team, called the Springboks. This was the team other nations had formally recognised and played against for a hundred years until isolation in the 1980s.

Between 2000 and 2010 the Proteas became the number one ranked test nation in the world three times. However, each time they achieved world number one their performance dipped, and the ranking was lost within months. From a performance perspective, the Proteas had the talent to be the best team in the world but could not sustain performances to stay at the top. The question was, why?

The Proteas may be the most diverse team in international sport. On any given game day, the team of eleven players can include indigenous Africans, Afrikaners, ethnic English and Indians; as well as Christians, Muslims and Hindus. This reflects the rich diversity of the 'Rainbow Nation', as well as the fact that selection policies are in place that prescribe a race-based quota.

The Proteas' team manager between 2008 and 2019 was Dr Mohammed Moosajee (Doc). Prior to that, Doc had been the team's doctor for five years. An outstanding schoolboy player himself, Doc had captained the non-white South African Schools team.

Doc describes the team culture in 2010 in this way:

'There was no unifying covenant to bind behaviour. There was a lack of a team identity. At that time, what we could become was undefined, unknown and untapped. Focus for the team was very much on the technical, tactical and physical aspects of the game.'

A number of inhibitors lay behind this inability to stay at the top. There had been a pattern of non-white players struggling to establish themselves at the start of their careers. Not feeling they belonged.

One such example was Hashim Amla who would later become one of the nation's greatest players. Hash was the nation's first Muslim international player and the first player of Indian origin to play test cricket for South Africa, his grandparents having migrated from Gujarat in India. In 2014, he would become the first non-white player to captain his country in test cricket.

However, in his first experience with the Proteas Hash found it difficult to fit into the team and as a result struggled to access his talent on the field.

Hash is a devout Muslim and his religious practices (such as daily prayers, Ramadan observance, halal food and his long traditional beard) were new to many of his teammates. Hash doesn't drink alcohol as its consumption is contrary to Islamic scripture.

Prior to making his debut, Hash 'humbly appealed' to Cricket South Africa that he be allowed to wear the national shirt without the beer sponsor's logo on it. Hash's request became a massive public issue and a predictably heated debate ensued. He was heavily criticised by some, even called 'arrogant'.

To their credit, Cricket South Africa and the beer sponsor acceded to Hash's request. However, this setting was far from ideal for a humble and gentle person such as Hash to walk into a complex team for the first time.

This sense of being an outsider was exacerbated by the team not having articulated a sense of purpose or identity that could bind the players together.

The culture at that time was, as former All Blacks captain

Anton Oliver explained, one where a sense of belonging, or 'true acceptance', was only obtained through proving yourself on the field over a long time, and in the meantime living with a sense of feeling 'second class, excluded'.

Walking into this setting, Hash averaged only ten runs per innings at the start of his career. He was then dropped.

Hash was recalled to the team over a year later. Better prepared for the experience of surviving in the team, Hash was able to adapt and perform. By the end of his career he would average 46 runs per innings over 124 test matches. He holds many records. He once scored 311 in a test match against England at the Oval. However, all of that could have easily been lost.

In early 2010, Doc Moosajee, the Proteas' captain Graeme Smith and team psychologist Jeremy Snape, a former England international, sat down to work out a way to address the team culture and explore how it could be transformed into a competitive advantage. In Jeremy's words:

> 'The environment was heavily focused on being busy – the physical, the technical, the tactical – which won a lot of games, but to build sustained success a different energy is required. It had to come from a more emotional place.'

The Proteas' inability to sustain excellence makes sense from a hormonal point of view. Our dopamine system is anticipatory. We receive bursts in the pursuit of a goal rather than on the attainment of it. These bursts increase when the outcome is uncertain as opposed to guaranteed.[53] This explains why we can feel so flat immediately after a major event or performance.

A flaw in the Proteas' team culture was that their 'purpose' had been confused with achieving a strategic outcome: the number one world ranking. This was motivating for the team but once they had achieved it the dopamine levels and motivation fell away. They felt flat and their performances deteriorated.

The Proteas needed a higher purpose than a ranking to maintain their motivation and focus.

Jeremy directed his attention to the Proteas' symbol itself as a potential source of this missing emotional edge. In his eighteen months with the team he had seen a superficial connection to the 'badge': a campaign strapline of *100% Pure Protea* painted across the team bus and on advertising billboards. Players scoring a century in a match kissed the Protea badge on their shirts or helmets, but what meaning did playing for this team really hold for them?

On a winter's day in 2010, Jeremy started the process of re-imagining the Proteas' team culture with a visit to Kirstenbosch National Botanical Gardens, under Table Mountain in Cape Town. Jeremy bought a book about the protea flower and walked around the gardens. He read of the Greek origins of the name and of the protea flower's unique qualities.

The team leadership, with the support of Cricket South Africa Chief Executive Gerald Majola, agreed that a camp should be convened to address the culture of the team. The venue would be a bush area on the banks of Hennops River in the Transvaal. I was approached to help facilitate the camp.

Creating a space to discuss the team's identity and purpose was not without risk, given the charged political tensions within South Africa. Doc Moosajee reflects back now:

'We knew there were risks in getting these issues on the table, but we had no choice if we wanted to get better. Sometimes these types of camps and offsites are really predetermined and the outcome manipulated. At Hennops River, none of us knew what would emerge or could predict the outcome. What was needed was genuine emotion that could unlock answers.'

Jeremy also felt there was no choice if the team wanted to get close to its potential:

'Yes, there were risks in holding these discussions but I knew that the team couldn't develop trust without transparency. The team's usual response was to either bottle things up and let the tension build or to channel their aggression into competition. To confront this underlying barrier to performance, we knew things would need to get messy before they could get better.'

I was also conscious of these risks. After all, this was one of the best teams in the world. It was not a basket case where a complete transformation was the easy option. Performance could be impaired by an unsuccessful camp, at least in the short term. Could this group of people deal with the issues that were going to be brought into the open? Would they even accept there was a fragility in their culture? Nobody knew the answers to those questions beforehand.

Our evolutionary story marks purpose as the starting point for any tribe, so this was where we started.

In the Proteas' context this was not straightforward. First, the team represented a nation that had historically never had a shared sense of purpose, or held a shared identity or shared vision of the future. Second, in our pre-camp surveying of the team there was a clear divide in player motivation. Some disclosed that they felt they were mostly playing for themselves. Others, that they were playing for their families and the ethnic or religious community they felt they most belonged to.

The approach we took in designing the camp was to not fear emotion.

What we wanted to avoid was a safe, rational discussion followed by false harmony and a set of words that made discomfort go away. We also needed to give voice to everyone present. That feeling was not going to be easy to generate for a nation who had for decades organised itself around inequality and division. As Doc Moosajee had identified, emotion was the only option for unlocking deep-seated feelings and underlying issues.

Inside a large traditional-style hut made of clay and wood, the first morning of the camp broke heavy with tension.

We started with a short film we'd produced, narrated by captain Graeme Smith, to set the scene. The film included a diverse range of ordinary people speaking to camera saying, 'You represent me'. The film also included Nelson Mandela introducing the concept of *ubuntu*.

The players were then given their national team shirts and asked to write on them what it personally meant to play for the Proteas. There followed an opportunity to stand before the team, read out what they had written and speak to its meaning. This enabled the players themselves to bring the emotion into the circle as well as surfacing the divergent motivations among them.

The touchpaper needed to ignite the players confronting these issues was a short reflection on the protea as a symbol for the team. In Jeremy Snape's words, this was the time for it to 'get messy'.

Jeremy introduced this part by explaining the many layers of the protea flower as a symbol. He explained how the name protea itself comes from Greek mythology and the story of Proteus, the son of Poseidon. Proteus' magical gift was to know the truth about the past, the present and the future.

Jeremy explained how the casing of the protea seed was fire-proof. When there was a bush fire the protea seed survived and was the first life to regenerate.

Having lived in South Africa for several years, Jeremy knew that gathering around a fire was a powerful social anchor for South Africans, so this link was an important hook in the story.

This conversation was enriched by the knowledge of one of the new players in the team, Colin Ingram, who had grown up on a protea farm. Colin's contribution was also important as a signal for an open floor as opposed to the discussion being dominated by those in the team with high status.

The punchline was clear: this was an incredible symbol and the team had not even scratched the surface of it.

Then the difficult conversations really began, as we asked the players for their honest feelings of the protea as their emblem.

Some spoke of enormous pride in this new national symbol. Some spoke of it feeling flat and without real meaning to them. Others even said that their families still spoke of the Springboks (the name of the all-white national team prior to the Proteas). This admission by some players, that their families never spoke of the Proteas but used the apartheid-era name for the team, sent shock waves through the room. I saw this as a predictable response to a team that had an identity vacuum.

Some players then spoke up and challenged what they perceived as a lack of buy-in to a post-apartheid Proteas team. This debate enabled a member of staff to challenge the team chant of '*bokke bokke bokke*', that was ritually sung after a match was won, as an uncomfortable and unwanted artefact of the apartheid era. Some spoke of feeling 'shame' in hearing that chant. Silence fell as the room absorbed this venting of raw honest emotion.

The divisiveness of the past was brought to life in a discussion in front of the team between acting head coach Corrie van Zyl and Doc Moosajee. They discussed the last test match played by the Springboks, in February 1990, against an unofficial England team. At that time, Corrie was a leading player in South Africa while Doc was a medical student. While that cricket match was being played, Doc was one of the protesters outside the ground who were dispersed by tear gas, bustled into a van and taken to police cells. The following day the rest of that series was cancelled and, on that very same day, Nelson Mandela was released from prison. Now, both Corrie and Doc were leaders in the Proteas' environment.

For most of the staff and the players, this was the first time they would have heard such a conversation between two men on different sides of the apartheid divide, recounting events through their opposing experiences. Parts of that discussion would have been highly uncomfortable for some. For others, even just talking about these issues in this way was liberating and perhaps even life-changing. What was crucial was the belief of these two men that the Proteas represented something much better than what had gone before. It was time to move on.

We avoided forcing any resolution or false harmony that afternoon. For a way forward to be authentic and have real meaning the players would need some time to find that themselves. Instead, the tense discussion was allowed to breathe and not revisited until the following day.

A critical element of the design of the camp was to bring in a wise ancestor, Ahmed Kathrada, on that first day. For he had suffered under the previous regime but had a calm, reassuring and optimistic view of the nation's future.

Ahmed was the bridge between the turbulence that had come to the surface that morning and a stronger culture in the future.

Ahmed was born in South Africa in 1929, the son of immigrant parents from India. From his teenage years, Ahmed resisted the discriminatory policies in the country and was at various times imprisoned for civil disobedience. Eventually he joined the African National Congress movement and in 1964 was accused of sabotage and attempting to overthrow the Government in the Rivonia Trial, along with others such as Nelson Mandela and Walter Sisulu. Ahmed was found guilty and sentenced to life imprisonment.

For the next eighteen years Ahmed was imprisoned in Robben Island maximum security prison. For much of that time, he shared a small cell with Nelson Mandela. In 1982 Ahmed and Mandela were transferred to Pollsmoor maximum security prison, where Ahmed stayed until released in 1989. In 1994 he became a Member of Parliament.

In his soft voice, Ahmed described his experiences in a way that no one present had ever heard before. Although his story was set within a brutal struggle, Ahmed, who was eighty years old when he visited us, seemed completely future-focused, not held back or bitter as a result of the persecution he had suffered.

He personified resilience and forgiveness and optimism and shone a light down a path the team could follow. The past needed to be farewelled and a future visioned that revolved around a shared purpose and identity. Hashim Amla later reflected:

'Because we had come out of isolation, the history . . . is not long, and it's also divided, so I am sure the country didn't even know its identity. We tried to understand what is a South African, because the Proteas team has to be the identity of the South African people.'[54]

Throughout this process, a word that kept recurring was *ubuntu*.

This had originally come from Nelson Mandela's voice in the short film we had shown at the start of the day. The players wanted to know more about this word, this idea. We listened again to the words of Nelson Mandela and Archbishop Desmond Tutu as they defined *ubuntu* in their own ways.

The team held and moulded *ubuntu* over those days of the Hennops River camp. They came to define it for themselves as *the measure of our lives is our impact on others*. This became the shared purpose upon which the 'Protea Fire Culture' was built. The metaphor of a mirror for *ubuntu* emerged – when all of the people of South Africa looked at this team, they were really looking at themselves. They were looking at their diversity working together, as brothers, towards a common cause.

One day a black brother may be the hero and the others celebrate that. The next day it may be a Muslim . . . the next day a white player . . . and so on. It did not matter who was the hero as they were kin. This was the impact the team could have on the nation. This was their purpose beyond the scoreboard or world rankings. The motivation to win was not diminished in the slightest. What was different was that in winning they would serve a higher purpose than a KPI. Hash again:

> 'The mirror of the country that you want to see is a team that is happy, a team that works together, a team where when you go through difficulties you are resilient, when you go through success you maintain your dignity in your success, and your failures. That is what you would like the country to be, and that is what we wanted the team to be and since 2010 we've tried to live that.'[55]

That evening the team ate together around the fire, known as the *boma* in South Africa. Just like their ancestors had done for millennia. The tensions of the day dissipated. A deeper feeling of belonging was building.

Due to the power of that day's event, from the *boma* that evening a sacred ritual emerged. In my time working with the team, I counted being part of eight such rituals, and all but once the team won their match the following day.

Sometimes it is the little things that become big things. After the tense discussion around Proteas vs Springboks, and feelings expressed about the '*bokke bokke bokke*' chant, one of the younger players, AB de Villiers, went away and composed a new chant made up of three national languages. The team still use this chant today. It is not surprising that, in time, AB became captain.

The next morning would always be critical with the heaviness of the previous day pushing into the new dawn.

The team breakfasted together in the bush over an open fire before returning to the traditional hut we'd spent the previous day in.

Before any of us had addressed the team, a player put his hand up to speak. Wrought with emotion, he said that yesterday's discussion around the team's identity and purpose had had a deep effect upon him. That he had not slept well. That he was one of the players whose family still referred to the team as the Springboks. That, before breakfast, he had called home and said, 'Father, I am not a Springbok – I am a Protea.'

It is rare that a team's cultural journey can have such a clear landmark moment. But this was one of the most important for the Proteas.

Much of the heavy tension in the hut lifted with this brave message. Without any prompting, other players, from all backgrounds, stood up to reaffirm the need to come together around a new Protea identity with *ubuntu* as its higher purpose. Doc Moosajee reflects:

'I could see straight away that the players felt they had more ownership in this team. That the protea was a symbol they all had a stake in. That *ubuntu* connected everyone. Previously, there were rules but not really unified standards. After Hennops River there became clarity in what it meant to be a Protea.'

That afternoon, without the team's prior knowledge, we took them to the local primary school in Hennops River. The school was comprised of roughly the same diversity proportions as the nation itself.

We had asked the head teacher whether she would arrange for her class of twelve-year-olds to give a lesson to the Proteas on the meaning of *ubuntu*. The students had spent weeks preparing for this moment. On the day they showed pure courage of their own, standing before their heroes and describing this ancient African spiritual idea of *ubuntu*. Then, in a very natural way, the students explained how watching the Proteas impacted on their own sense of being South African. From their mouths, it could not have been clearer that the scoreboard was not enough – that what they were seeking from this team was proof of what it was to be a South African.

When they looked at the team they were looking into a mirror.

3.4 renewal

There is no evidence of the soul except in its sudden absence. A nothingness enters, taking the place where something was before.

Bruce Springsteen in his memoir *Born to Run*

Over the four years that followed the Hennops River camp, the Proteas would almost continuously retain the number one test ranking in the world. A prolonged period of consistent high-level performances.

Sport is a dynamic and complex part of life where it is simply not possible to reduce success down to one isolated component. However, the transformation of the team culture undoubtedly contributed. AB de Villiers, who would go on to become one of the world's best players, reflects on the Hennops River camp:

'The uncertainty and insecurity you feel coming into any team was worse for us given our history as a nation. The Hennops River camp took us into a place of equality. Every individual belonged and was connected to a shared purpose. This allowed us to become more consistent as a team over the following years.'

Culture never stands still. Every day it shifts. How we deal with new situations redefines *who we really are* and *how we really do things*. When new people come into the environment and others leave, the dynamic changes. One of the great risks in sustaining a strong culture is when there is a transition between leaders.

By 2015 the Proteas had changed a lot. Captain Graeme Smith and other highly experienced players had gone. The coaches had changed. Jeremy Snape and I had left as well. The junior players at Hennops River had become senior players.

This new Proteas team had set their heart on winning the 2015 World Cup – not as an end in itself but as the most powerful expression of *ubuntu*. They saw a divided nation at home, and they wanted to bring it together and remind them of their shared identity and shared future.

The team was confident of success and playing well until narrowly beaten in the last over of their rain-affected semi-final against New Zealand in Auckland.

The loss was heartbreaking for the team on a number of levels. The nail-biting conclusion involved missed opportunities as the match came to its climax. Beyond factors on the field, the loss was further soured by perceived political interference in the selection of the team itself for the semi-final. Most of all, there was a sense of a failed mission to realise *ubuntu* in the way they had visioned.

The team was heartbroken.

Eighteen months on, the pain and scars were still there, and the team's performances fell away badly, losing matches they should have won.

The togetherness in the team had slipped and some previously strong relationships became strained as the pressure built.

In their despondency, the team had unconsciously drifted away from the Protea Fire Culture; the language had shifted away from purpose and identity and back to the physical, technical and tactical. Rituals had slipped.

Doc Moosajee was still the team manager and he called time on this. Along with dual captains AB de Villiers and Faf du Plessis, a second culture camp was convened. This time at Fairway near Pretoria. I was invited back to help again.

By the time of this second camp the Proteas had fallen from the number one ranking in the world to number seven.

The Fairway camp created space for a fresh reconnection to the foundations of the Protea Fire Culture.

The stories told at Hennops River were retold. This was important as two-thirds of the team in 2016 had not been at the 2010 camp. These players got to hear the deep meaning that underpinned the team's culture.

In my experience, once a strong culture is set it's essential that its foundations and relevance are regularly revisited by the team. Ideally, this is done before each new season or campaign. Some teams ritually do this, taking time out of training and often incorporating a shared experience.

The Proteas waiting six years to reconnect with their cultural foundations was too long and cultural drift had set in, reflected in their performance levels having fallen away.

It was important not to impose anything on this new generation of players at Fairway. After the stories were retold, I facilitated a discussion on whether the Protea Fire Culture still represented the team's purpose, identity and values. The players unanimously agreed that they believed it did.

However, in significant ways the younger generation redefined some of the language. For example, the younger players wanted to adopt a more aggressive and proactive way of playing. They felt this represented an emerging attitude in wider society.

In this discussion, co-captain AB de Villiers provided remarkable insight by explaining that the team's traditional defensive approach was probably influenced by the Afrikaners' '*laager* mentality'. AB explained how, long ago, white settlers trekking into new areas would at night form their wagons into a circle to defend against raiders and nocturnal predators. This defensive formation became embedded in the Afrikaners' own Us story when the *laager* was used to defeat much greater sized armies which attacked them.

This was a powerful example of one culture safely educating another on how they saw the world and how that influenced their mindset and strategic thinking. Even more impressively, AB and Faf were able to listen to the new generation and buy into their desire to evolve the team's approach.

In this way, the team's values evolved and moved forward.

Following this reconnection to the cultural foundations, specific issues in the team were allowed to surface. Some of these were dealt with by the team as a whole, such as ongoing tensions caused by the race quota policy. Others were dealt with by the leadership group, including a lack of alignment at crucial times. Other issues were dealt with privately by individuals themselves.

The team then invoked *ubuntu* to reset their collective goals for the following few years.

Faf du Plessis reflects back on the 2016 Fairway camp in this way:

'A safe platform to speak was made. The angst and frustration and anger in the team was allowed to surface. In this team it is so important to hear all the different perspectives. Working through all that allowed us to return to our purpose and identity as a team. We became healthy again. The success that followed over the next few years came about because we understood our "why" again.'

Within six months of the Fairway camp the Proteas had rebounded from seventh back to world number one.

My time with the Proteas ended in early 2019. Over that decade the Protea Fire Culture continued over four different coaching regimes under Corrie van Zyl, Gary Kirsten, Russell Domingo (the Proteas' first head coach of colour) and Ottis Gibson (its first black coach).

In the last Proteas camp I attended I saw the same ritual for new players that was born in Hennops River ten years earlier. New players sat on bar stools in front of the team and a senior player acted as MC. *Welcome. We do not judge you by how you perform tomorrow. You belong here. Just be yourself.* There followed three time-honoured questions for each new player to answer in front of their new teammates. The last one of which is, *What impact does it have on others that you are a Protea?*

Ubuntu.

Players talk about their families, their communities, their schools, their mentors. Therein, personal meaning becomes attached to the shared purpose.

In that final camp I attended, only two players remained from the Hennops River camp a decade earlier. But the same rituals of belonging and purpose were being repeated and the emotion had never been stronger.

Many players and staff who came into the Proteas during these years have had their perceptions of the world transformed by sharing time and space with such a diverse group; different cultures coming together and forming a new way of being – true modern South Africans.

I recall scenes in the dressing room where a tall, lanky Afrikaner player would be stretching over a Muslim kneeling in prayer as he tried to get something out of his locker. These moments were pure and transcended sport. They had learned each other's ways, and these had become normal to them. As with the All Blacks, the Proteas would leave the team with a kinder and more enlightened understanding of the society they were part of.

The ongoing power of *ubuntu* in the Proteas' team culture was evident on my last evening in Port Elizabeth. As the sun had begun to set, we took a bus into the centre of that city. It was dinner time. There, we joined three inspirational volunteers who, every evening, fed homeless people outside the city's train station. The players helped plate the food and then took it to the hundred or so homeless people waiting for their meal. They handed them the plates of food, then sat with them and chatted while they ate. No mention of this was ever made to the media. All that mattered to the team that evening was the impact they could have on these people they represented.

Ubuntu.

3.5 the mission

It always seems impossible, until it is done.

— Nelson Mandela

Defining a team's purpose seems to have become unnecessarily complicated and convoluted.

Homo sapien's evolutionary story unequivocally tells us that the purpose of groups is to promote the wellbeing of their people.

That's it.

For most of human history this higher purpose has been translated by tribes into a mission to simply survive – *feed the village*. That has until relatively recently been a constant daily, weekly, seasonal struggle for most *homo sapiens*. Survival is still the day-to-day mission of many tribes in the world, including many businesses. Survival means mouths are fed. It allows the venture to continue. It is a noble cause.

There is also the emotional wellbeing of a tribe in the sense of individual and collective self-esteem and the frequency and intensity of experiences of feelings of belonging, stress, sadness and love.

'Success' of a group is an illusion without these core wellbeing markers being met.

In so many endeavours today, from sport to business, we see the achievement of an outcome at the cost of broken people. That is not the definition of success we inherited from our ancestors. Rather, that is us having lost our way, led by ego rather than the welfare of others.

How the higher purpose of protecting the tribe's wellbeing is converted into a practical mission is highly contextual.

For the ancient Polynesian navigators, a thousand years ago, the life they had enjoyed for many generations had become unsustainable on their tiny island in the centre of the Pacific Ocean. In order to deliver the higher purpose of protecting their people, they needed to dramatically change their mission. So, they went exploring for new lands for their descendants to survive and then thrive in. The discoveries of Hawaii and New Zealand followed.

The next question is, *Who is our tribe?* For a government or national sports team, it is all the people they represent. For a self-employed person it may be their family waiting at home.

For the Proteas, their tribe is beyond the playing team – it is the South African 'Rainbow Nation'. Their purpose, captured by *ubuntu*, is to promote the wellbeing of their people by giving them inspiration, confidence and a blueprint of how diverse cultures can work and live together as brothers and sisters.

For small businesses I have worked with, their tribe may be defined at the start as the founders. Their mission is survival. Once their viability is established they then move to making the enterprise sustainable over the medium term. As the business evolves their definition of their tribe widens to include employees and customers.

In *whakapapa* terms, as the sun arrives on each generation this higher purpose is passed on to them and they ask the question of themselves: *What do we need to do to promote the wellbeing of our people?* Therein lies their mission.

In Abu Dhabi, I found a dramatic example of how, over time, a constant higher purpose can translate into vastly different missions. It resonated with me because the story of that nation parallelled that of my own tribe *Ngāi Tahu*.

In 2015 I was retained by the City Football Group as they sought to align their three principal football investments at that time: Manchester City, New York City and Melbourne City. In this project I spent time with each of the teams in their respective cities. The challenge was to culturally and strategically align such diverse clubs, while at the same time respecting their unique local senses of identity.

The work started with a visit to Abu Dhabi to immerse myself in the strategy and culture of the owners.

Until 1958, Abu Dhabi was one of the most impoverished countries in the Middle East. Generations had endured a harsh climate, a scarcity of water and food, neighbours fighting over its borders and British occupation.

Theirs was a subsistence life, moving with the seasons. The country's only real export was pearls. The occupation of pearling was gruelling and dangerous. Boats were at sea for months at a time, with boys diving from twelve years of age. The pearl divers dived all daylight hours, eating only in the evening, their skin and eyes damaged by the saltwater and sun. The rest of the year they farmed nomadically. It was a hard life.

Prior to 1958, Abu Dhabi had one (religious) school for boys, no doctors, no medical facilities, and an estimated illiteracy rate of 98 per cent.

The nation's higher purpose of protecting the wellbeing of the people was translated into a constant struggle for survival.

However, there was a deep-seated belief, passed on by each generation, that their mission would change. That, one day, an event would occur that would deliver them from this harsh adversity. When that time arrived, the mission for that generation of leaders would transform from survival to seizing the opportunity to lock in lasting care for the people (medical care, education, houses, free-flowing water, electricity, comforts). New generations were told to be ready.

When oil was discovered within Abu Dhabi in 1958, that moment of opportunity had arrived:

As a people, we had been patient, resilient and hopeful for a long time ... keeping alive our belief in a destiny which included prosperity for all. Despite the pain and deprivation we suffered we trusted there would be light at the end of the tunnel and we continued to seek that light.[56]

Their higher purpose remained the same, but the mission had dramatically changed: *It fell on our generation to fulfil the dreams of our forefathers.*

Through the leadership of Sheikh Zayed that is exactly what they did. From the mid-1960s, the nation went from without to world-class hospitals, schools, electrification and infrastructure. Citizens were given cash and granted land for homes and to build businesses. Abu Dhabi is one of the wealthiest nations in the world today but they do not judge themselves on that; they measure themselves against the mission they set to deliver their higher purpose.

This pattern of a constant higher purpose expressed through changing missions reflects the experience of my own tribe *Ngāi Tahu*. From the time of large-scale European settlement in the mid-1800s land was wrongly transferred from the guardianship of our tribe to the private ownership of individuals and the Government itself. This constituted a breach of the 1840 treaty between indigenous tribes and the British Crown.

In 1998 the Government formally apologised to *Ngāi Tahu* and paid reparations of 170 million dollars. Just over twenty years later the tribe's total assets amount to over one and a half billion dollars. With the treaty settlement, the tribe's mission shifted from a subsistence existence to investing in infrastructure and programmes that will ensure the long-term wellbeing of the people.

Across these distant tribes, no matter what the day brings, their constant north star is the wellbeing of their people.

4

vision-driven

Where there is no vision, the people perish.

Proverbs 29:18

4.1 the navigator

Not all those who wander are lost.

J.R.R. Tolkien

We are a vision-driven species. As Professor Robin Dunbar puts it, 'We trust what we see above every other sense.' We are designed to see what is in front of us and imagine what comes after.

A thousand years ago ancient Polynesian navigators embarked on the greatest sea voyaging known to man.

This came about by converting their higher purpose into a vision of what they could accomplish. Herein lay the mission they would embark upon. Once the vision was clear, it was translated into a plan that was successfully executed one task at a time. This remains our template for great accomplishments.

The pursuit of its vision was a sacred experience for the tribe. The precise destination was unknown – it lay outside their knowledge; what mattered was the aspiration and the pictures they painted of what could be. The detail of the journey would reveal itself as they went.

These epic voyages originated from a group of tiny islands in the central Pacific Ocean. The heart of this prolific voyaging was the island of Ra'iātea, a mere sixty-four square miles, that is today part of the Society Islands within French Polynesia. Ra'iātea is my tribe's spiritual homeland. The place, it is said, that our souls return to after our death.

In this narrow window of around five hundred years, these ancient navigator ancestors would explore over ten million square miles, 25 per cent of the Earth's surface. These voyages were undertaken in double-hulled canoes, *waka*, or *va'a* to our Hawaiian cousins, up to sixty feet long. They made their vision into reality without maps or instruments or a written language.

To the north, our ancestors discovered and populated the Hawaiian islands. To the south, the great navigator Kupe was the first to discover the southern islands now known as New Zealand. His wife, Kuramārōtini, who joined him on this voyage, named these islands *Aotearoa* (Land of the Long White Cloud).

After his discovery, Kupe navigated his way back to those tiny islands in the Central Pacific and shared the attainment of their mission. Subsequent generations set forth a great fleet of their own voyaging canoes, one of which, the *Takitimu*, contained my ancestors. The great fleet followed Kupe's navigational directions to the southern islands where they would settle and become the Māori.

For many years European experts cast doubt on whether the Polynesian navigators discovered new lands with purpose and skill. It was claimed that these epic discoveries were accidental – the result of currents and trade winds. Recent scientific studies, computer modelling and a deeper understanding of ancient navigational techniques have borne out the stories passed down to us and settled the question.[57]

The navigators' strength came from their ability to simultane-ously carry in their hands both a grand vision and an intimate understanding of the detail. The sun. The stars. Constellations. Polaris. The Southern Cross. The sea currents. The thirty-two different types of ocean swells. The meaning of cloud types over land and ocean. The causes of the shifting colours of the water. The feeding habits of seabirds. The migratory patterns of whales, albatrosses, dolphins and turtles.

Each *waka* was led by a navigator who guided the vessel and its people. The navigator was the guardian of the tribe's culture on these voyages. A sacred part of the vision was how the people would retain their sense of identity as they pursued the mission. The navigator took with them the tribe's Us story, and the stones that represented their values, as they wrote the next chapter.

The Us stories were literally carved into the wooden hull of the vessel. An ornate carved godly head at the front acting as their guardian.

In constructing the vessels, the sacredness of the mission was evident in how they treated the trees chosen for the purpose. These trees were deemed living ancestors; they had shared the land and breath with generations of their kin. Trees were blessed before being felled and hollowed. Our ancestors foresaw the inev-itable adversity ahead and took comfort that the heart of these great trees was not at their centre, but rather to the side that had faced the harshest force of nature. They understood that the most beautiful patterns in these trees resided in the places that had suffered the most.

The navigator understood that the voyaging had to take place between winter and summer when the winds would be best and the stars most strongly aligned to guide them. All of this detail was essential to convert the vision into reality.

Once the visioning was done and the mission set, the ancient navigators were ready. They would say, *Now, let the islands come to us.*

Five hundred years later, on another great ocean, Christopher Columbus voyaged with the same vision-driven intent as my ancestors: *Following the light of the sun, we left the Old World . . .*[58] Columbus pursued a vision of a 'New World'.

Our navigator ancestors can be found all over the world. My Muslim brothers speak of the great Bedouin navigators, in the Arabian Peninsula, who did not use any devices or maps either. They used the sun in the day and the stars in the night to navigate. Instead of sea swells, they gained direction from the way the winds sculptured the shape of dunes.[59]

Our ancestors deeply understood this power of imagination, of visioning, of creating mental models to guide us. They were masters at ensuring that everyone was aligned as they moved towards their shared vision.

Visioning is another essential ingredient in our super strength of creating strong teams. However, what was intuitive to our ancestors has become weakened over time by tasks disconnected from meaning. This is demonstrated by how many contemporary leaders start with a strategy rather than working from purpose to vision to mission and then to a plan.

That would be a truly foreign land to our ancient navigator ancestors. Studies have reported that only 3 per cent of leaders' time today is spent on visioning but that three in four workers expect their leaders to paint pictures of the future.[60] The people still have this primal need for a vision, but are too often let down by those charged to guide them.

Whatever the diversity within a team, what they most tangibly share is the future they are about to embark on together.

4.2 foresight

The science is catching up with our ancestors. We now better understand our reliance on 'seeing' to understand the world around us. Where our images go, our energy follows.

The part of the human brain responsible for processing visual information is the largest, covering more than 50 per cent of its surface.[61] Vision gives us the richest detail to assess threats and opportunities and, as a species, our eyesight is second only to birds of prey.

Our ideas relating to vision have had a profound impact on how we feel about the world around us. We have translated the ideas of lightness and darkness into symbols for safety and fear, into knowledge and ignorance, and into good and bad.

Crucially, our understanding of 'seeing' is not limited to the physical act of processing visual information. The definition of 'vision' itself encompasses both the physical act of seeing, and a thought formed by the imagination or something 'seen' in a dream. In both cases, our brains give equal weight to what we see before us and what we imagine.

Our ability to imagine is central to the human condition. When we vision, either seeing or imagining, and each time we consistently return to the vision, we are hardwiring neural pathways. Put another way, we are creating forward memories. As science writer David Hamilton shared:

Researchers at Harvard University, led by Alvaro Pascual-Leone, compared the brains of people playing a sequence of notes on a piano with the brains of people imagining playing the notes. The region of the brain connected to the finger muscles was found to have changed to the same degree in both groups of people, regardless of whether they struck the keys physically or mentally.[62]

Elite performers have long taken advantage of this insight and mentally rehearsed their performances through visualisation.

Visualisation strengthens, with repetition, the myelin insulation of neural pathways that performers can lock into during their actual performance. The more insulation around these neural pathways, the faster the information transmits in real time between brain and muscles, to the point of becoming automatic.

So, in the event itself, and especially in high-anxiety moments, we have a preformed response and minimal need to consciously think through our actions. Our ability to deliver our talent is freed up, even when there is high scrutiny or distraction around us. We have previewed and practised the response we want, and it is waiting for us.

Performance psychologist Michael Gervais is highly skilled in teaching visualisation to elite performers:

'The visualisation process needs to be as real as possible to fire this system. Not just vision but all senses if possible. It requires a disciplined approach of embodying and experiencing lifelike images.'

Visioning a goal activates our (feel-good) dopamine system that sustains our motivation and focus.

The more emotional weight attached to a vision, the stronger these neural pathways will be. Our ancestors intuitively understood that visioning has to be tied to a tribe's Us story. This is where the necessary emotional heft came from.

It is paradoxical that elite individual performers are so proficient at visualisation, yet it is rare to find teams that are similarly skilled and practised at doing this collectively with comparable intent or depth. Therein lies a lost opportunity for aligning everyone in pursuit of a desired outcome.

All too often in teams, visioning is replaced by the imposition of abstract words, strategy or a linear outcome. None of which can be easily visualisable. This invites misalignment and diluted motivation.

In my work I've found producing bespoke films of the team's identity and vision particularly effective. This visual stimulus along with activation of imagination packs the most punch. I have mostly worked with Joel Mishcon and Stephen Parker of Chrome Productions on these films.

An example of such a film we made together was in 2016 for Ford Motor Company in Detroit. The film was produced for that year's 24 Hours of Le Mans motor race. This was Ford's return to Le Mans fifty years after beating Ferrari in an epic encounter recreated in the 2019 film *Ford v Ferrari*. One of the performance challenges for Ford in 2016 was that its drivers had never raced together before and would likely not do so again. This would be a one-off experience for this particular group of people. The drivers were world class but without shared experience or a baked-in sense of belonging.

The five-minute film we made includes footage of Henry Ford himself a hundred years ago and his story of racing cars to generate enough income to keep developing his designs. The film then shifts to footage of the epic 1966 race, including images of Henry Ford II. As we shift to today, current Ford President Bill Ford appears in the boardroom looking to camera. Then images preview the race itself. The film's sentiment is captured in the lines at the end: '*The race is calling us again, our ancestors are waiting there ahead of us, respecting this part of the journey is ours.*'

The film was loved by the team and staff (and unknown to me at the time, went on to win a film-making award). It is called *Into the Heart* and can be found on YouTube.[63] It was terrific to sit back and watch the team win the race again that year in another memorable head-to-head clash with Ferrari.

Of course, some elite leaders are outstanding in how they facilitate collective visioning in their tribe. We will meet some in this chapter. They toggle between the first-person perspective to make it personal, and then switch to a third-person viewpoint, a helicopter view, to try and insert as much objectivity as possible. Zooming in and zooming out of the vision.

An ancestral example I've explored with teams is Roald Amundsen and Robert Falcon Scott's 1911 race to be the first to reach the South Pole. Both men, and their teams, with the same goal in the same brutal environment.

Much has been written about how Amundsen's team prevailed by thirty-four days over Scott's, arriving back at base on the precise day they had forecast. The outcome made more poignant by Scott and his team perishing on their attempt to return to base.

Much has been written about the superiority of Amundsen's preparation and leadership to Scott's. What may have been underestimated in Amundsen's success is how he deployed visioning with his team.

On the voyage from Norway on Amundsen's ship, the *Fram*, there was a map of Antarctica on a wall, with the planned route marked in red. This was a constant reference point. Navigation sheets for the route were handed to the team to study. Together, they discussed the expedition and agreed on a tactic of fifteen miles per day whatever the conditions. Each day of that long sea voyage Amundsen's team were visioning the path they would take.

In contrast, Scott adopted a command and control approach where much of the information was withheld from the team. In fact, the strategy for the expedition was not determined until his ship, the *Terra Nova*, had arrived in Antarctica. Even then, the route and tactics were not disclosed to the wider team until they had set off across the snow. Those plans then changed many times as their logistics unravelled, including a mechanised sledge that failed. There was no 'fifteen-mile march' with Scott. Instead, influenced by gut instinct and weather forecasts, Scott decided each morning what they would pursue that day. Unlike Amundsen's relentless march, some days Scott would exceed fifteen miles but then others not travel at all, including six consecutive days staying in a tent during a harsh storm. Scott's approach caused stress and confusion in his team.

From a performance point of view, Amundsen's team had a clear competitive advantage before they even set foot on Antarctica. They could visualise the overall mission, key details of the landscape and how they would execute their plan. For

Scott's team, the desired outcome was clear but the way they would achieve it was a mystery they stepped into each day.

One modern disciple of our visioning tradition is Pete Carroll, Head Coach of the Seattle Seahawks NFL team, and one of my favourite coaches in sport. His success as one of only three coaches to have won both the NFL Super Bowl and a National College Championship (with the University of Southern California) has been vision-driven:

'If it was really good . . . what would it be like? There comes the vision . . . Now, it's just about staying connected to it. That is where the coach comes in. We keep you connected to the vision until it becomes true and lives . . .'

4.3 the gap

To see things in the seed, that is genius.

Lao Tzu

Whenever we reflect on our higher purpose, of promoting the wellbeing of our tribe, we see a gap between where we are today and where we could be. This is the seed of our vision.

At times, the tribe is doing well and the gap between our purpose and current reality seems relatively small. We are on the right path. Other times, the gap is so wide it seems an ocean away. Something more radical is required by those generations. They may have to reinvent themselves or find a new world.

For my Polynesian ancestors, their vision of discovering new islands came from a gap between their current reality (climatic change, overpopulation, tribal warring) and their higher purpose of promoting the welfare of their tribe. For those generations, their shared purpose demanded that they explore, that they move. This is where their epic voyaging emerged from.

One of the world's leading behavioural psychologists is Eric Blondeau. Eric works with elite athletes, such as Olympians, anti-terror police and hostage negotiators. I've been fortunate enough to work with him on a few projects.

Eric identifies how great leaders understand the power of

articulating this gap between current reality and how their purpose could be more impactfully delivered:

'Mandela, Churchill, Ghandi, Martin Luther King all understood that a shared vision changes behaviour. They were able to identify a collective frustration – the gap between current reality and where we want to be. From this came a vision to answer that frustration. We change vision, we change behaviour.'

On the one side, the status quo represents a gnawing frustration, a sense of failure or even anger. On the other side, there is the anticipation of what we don't yet have, something treasured but not guaranteed, an aspirational vision of what could be. It is emotive framing of a gap that releases dopamine and motivates individuals towards a shared goal.

In 2011 the NBA's Golden State Warriors found themselves in this exact position. They had missed the NBA playoffs for seventeen of the previous eighteen seasons. This was bordering on the statistically impossible in a salary cap competition where losing teams get the top draft picks the following year.

One of the key steps taken by the team's new ownership regime in 2011 was to recruit Rick Welts. Rick was appointed the President of the Golden State Warriors after previous leadership roles with the Phoenix Suns and the NBA head office itself.

From 2015, the Warriors would go to five consecutive NBA Finals, winning three of them, becoming the most dominant NBA team since Michael Jordan's Chicago Bulls in the 1990s.

Rick Welts came to the Warriors with a vision. That vision

provided the organisation with a bridge between its current reality and becoming a champion. As Rick put it:

'We had a culture of losing. We had an expectation every year of losing. We expected it on the court and in business.'[64]

On his first day with the Warriors, Rick Welts brought the staff together and set out a vision of success. He identified key markers along the way to this vision being realised. Welts' starting point was that the team should be one of the most successful franchises in all of sports. He told staff, 'It's all here, you've just got to believe it's all here.'[65]

Welts started with purpose: why success would benefit the diverse community of the city. He then gave reasons why such success was achievable: the advantages of their geographic location, robust fan affinity, the corporate base around the team and its internal resources. There followed an analysis of the cultural reasons why failure had persisted with the Warriors for so long. Then, the vision emerged:

'My first day in the office I brought everyone together and said, "This is what is going to happen" . . . we created the promise of what could be and made people believe the path to get there . . . small wins helped people believe the story was true.'[66]

Detail was provided of what was required to bridge the gap between persistent failure and future success. This included transformation of the Warriors' relationship with the NBA, re-imagining the connection with the Bay Area 'tribe' and an internal culture change.

The staff were given the option of either buying into the vision or checking out. Within eighteen months half of the staff had left. Those remaining in the *waka* moved forward together aligned by the shared vision.

Head Coach Steve Kerr translated this high-level organisational vision into one for the basketball team itself – in terms of both a style of play and a team culture that could win championships.

In his coaching, Steve Kerr, like Pete Carroll, strives to keep his players connected to the team's vision in every interaction they have (from meetings to practice to performing):

'What I try to do is to continue to communicate our vision and gently nudge guys along.'[67]

Navigators.

4.4 colouring in the detail together

The vision must be shared by the people. It is, after all, the path the tribe will travel together, and ultimately form their collective legacy.

There are clues that the ancient Polynesian navigators would eat together around the campfire the evening before they embarked on their great voyages. They would retell Us stories, of course. But something else occurred. The navigator would repeat the vision they were about to pursue one more time. Clarity and alignment deepened around the fire.

A thousand years later, such leadership skills may be diminishing. Instead of time taken to deepen the sharing of the vision, often what transpires is the dumping of a one-dimensional vision onto a team alongside a detailed strategy on how to deliver it.

The vision isn't given time to breathe, to take life, to be adopted by the people, for mental pictures to come into sight. Instead, with undue haste, the people's heads are down looking at the tactical and technical. The connection between the work and higher purpose breaks down.

In teams in which the vision is weak there is a narrowness in the work. Individuals focused on KPIs, disconnected from the big picture. Teams siloed from one another as they seek to complete their agendas. On a wider scale, the same phenomenon pervades politics. There are lots of policies, laws, regulations and measurements but they do not add up to a shared future we can visualise.

This approach to our work does not reflect the fact that we are biologically and psychologically a vision-driven species. It lacks humanity.

Our better leaders today, as with our ancestors in the past, stay with the visioning until it is full and the mental pictures clear and rich in detail. They co-create the vision with their team. They sketch a picture but then everyone together colours it in.

This process of collective 'colouring in' is not symbolic, but rather highly pragmatic. It is from this stage that a realistic and resilient strategy can emerge – the practical steps that will define our mission.

This detailed part of the visioning work requires a deep focus on the elements that we control. Eric Blondeau marries the tension between the big picture and the detail in this way:

'We live in a complex world where we lack control. Where we are influenced by many random events. We delude ourselves that we have control. So, when we think of the future, when we vision, it is important to not focus on outcome beyond our control but focus on those elements we can control.'

Eric highlights a key feature of high-performing teams: their discipline to keep their focus on those elements they are able to control (or at the very least, influence).

Our ancient navigator ancestors understood this interplay between the vision (such as finding a place of abundance that would sustain them and their descendants) and the many micro elements they could control on the journey there (such as how well they prepared, their intimate understanding of the 'seascape' and the wellbeing of the crew).

When I'm working with a team before a major campaign, we will draw a circle and stand around it. Inside the circle, we will identify the elements that we can control on our voyage: our preparation, our level of clarity, our behaviours, our connection with each other. Outside the circle, we will define those elements that we cannot control and could become distractions that drain our energy: the media, social media, the weather, how the competition is being regulated . . . We make a commitment to each other to stay disciplined around what we control.

A powerful example of enlightened leadership when it comes to constructing a shared vision comes from the Chicago Cubs baseball club.

It started with a gap . . . quite a big gap. The Cubs had last won the World Series in 1908. They would not win another National League title for 71 years and they would not win another World Series for 108 years. Both of those are record dry spells in major league baseball.

In 2011 the Cubs' management recruited Theo Epstein followed by Jed Hoyer and Jason McLeod to change their Us story. These three men had played pivotal roles in the Boston Red Sox overcoming their own historic 'curse' and finally winning the World Series again in 2004 (their first in eighty-six years) and then again in 2007.

As with the Red Sox, generations upon generations of Cubs fans, players, coaches and management had come and gone, unable to get back to the holy grail of the World Series.

The Cubs' new regime commenced with a gathering of staff

in the ballroom of a budget hotel in Masa, Arizona, a few weeks before Spring Training of 2012. The gathering lasted for three days.

Theo Epstein began by sketching out a vision of the Cubs winning their next World Series and then going on to compete for many more thereafter.

Epstein's vision was more than an outcome, it was three-dimensional: the type of baseball they would play, the type of players they needed athletically and in terms of character, the operational points of difference they would generate and how to create the best environment in baseball.[68]

Many modern leaders would stop here, hand out a strategy and tell everyone to go back to their offices and work hard on it.

That's not what this leadership team did. The visioning had only just begun, and the proper conversation hadn't even started. Theo Epstein went on:

'Now, it's up to us. That's the vision, we can all agree on that, now it's up to all of us to collectively figure out the [detail]. How are we going to get there? What's the journey going to look like?'

Over the course of the next three days, the staff would build the vision and identify the strategic detail around the idea of 'the Cubs' Way'. Epstein explains:

'That's when we met and talked about "the Cubs' Way" ... the room became a baseball think tank where no detail was too small to be debated.'[69]

The gathered staff were put into groups and were tasked with deep-diving into the high-level areas of the vision. As I call it, 'colouring in the detail'. Cubs General Manager Jed Hoyer told me:

'A top-down approach would not have worked. Just before we arrived important rule changes had come in and we had to pivot direction from the Red Sox experience. We had to re-imagine how the Cubs could be successful. We needed to do that with everyone.'

This collaborative approach sent a strong message to staff that the new leadership team was not arrogantly coming in with a so-called recipe for success cooked up in Boston.

The Cubs' Way became the map followed in pursuit of this vision of bringing more World Series titles back to Wrigley Field. Within this collaborative vision new standards of excellence emerged, clarity of style of play, how they wanted to teach the game to their players, the type of people they wanted in the clubhouse – all amounting to a transformed organisational identity.

Everyone fed in and contributed. The output shared and debated. Over the coming weeks it was consolidated into a 259-page document called 'The Cubs' Way' which remains a guiding artefact for the organisation today. The document is prefaced with a simple statement: *Our mission is to help the Chicago Cubs win the World Championship.* The content, constructed by all staff, formed a bridge between their inherited reality and what could be possible.

As the team was rebuilt over the following few years the players took on the vision and coloured it in for themselves. One of the elements the players visioned was an incredible victory parade in the city after claiming their first World Series in over a hundred years. The moment when their undying loyal fans would be rewarded with a trophy to celebrate. The poignancy in visualising such a parade lay in the fact that the generations before them, their ancestors going back to 1908, had been denied such a moment.

On 2 November 2016, within the timeframe they had envisioned in that staff gathering four years earlier, the Cubs beat the Cleveland Indians in Cleveland by eight runs to seven in extra innings in the deciding game seven of the World Series.

Two days later, the victory parade through the streets of downtown Chicago took place, just as the team had visioned. It has been estimated that over five million fans attended the parade, more than the total population of Chicago, and reportedly the seventh largest gathering in human history.

As Jed Hoyer explained the Cubs' visioning and strategising process to me, it mirrored three elements I had seen across other high-performing teams:

First, a gap between higher purpose and current reality was identified. What was clear from the Cubs' story was how winning another World Series would enhance the wellbeing of their tribe – long-suffering fans, as well as those players who strove before them, and past owners too. Yes, winning would bring personal and familial benefits, but the Cubs had a clear focus on bringing another World Series title to a much wider tribe of stakeholders.

Second, the Cubs built the vision and then layered it with the whole team – *they coloured it in together*. What became clear in this process was a desire to build a perennially competitive club, not a one-off event.

Third, as the detail of the vision was coloured in, there came the strategic plan – the Cubs' Way – that would guide the mission with its deep focus on what was within their control.

4.5 rehearsing adversity

Micronesian ocean navigator Mau Piailug, who as a teacher resurrected traditional wayfinding navigation in the Pacific in the 1970s, had an expression: 'fair weather does not make a master'.[70]

This positive attitude to adversity reflects what is known as a 'challenge mindset', as opposed to a 'threaten mindset'. Many studies have identified a 'challenge mindset' as a distinguishing feature of elite performers and teams. Leading performance psychologist Professor Marc Jones explains:

> 'In a challenge state an individual recognises that the situation is important, believes success is possible and thinks they have sufficient resources to meet the demands. In this state, an individual is able to maintain performance, and even perform optimally under stress and adversity.'

A key aspect of building a 'challenge mindset' is time spent rehearsing adversity so that if / when it arises, it is already part of the mental pictures we have painted into our vision.

Again, we do this through the discipline of staying focused on what we can control. Whilst the cause of adversity may fall outside our influence, our response is something we control. This is what we rehearse and integrate into our vision.

When Michael Gervais works with elite athletes, they typically spend around 85 per cent of visualisation time previewing them executing their plans and the remaining 15 per cent of time anticipating and responding to potential disrupters.

When working with teams, that ratio is something I also employ. We will spend most of our time previewing how we want to deliver our performance and then a small but important amount of time on scenarios previewing adversity.

The need for this work was brought home to me when working with a club which had put together a new coaching team. In the new head coach's urgency to get started with the players and the pre-season, no time had been carved out to rehearse adversity.

One potential source of adversity I had raised was the fact that the new coaching team had not worked together before nor did most of them know each other well as people. What could be foreseen was misunderstandings and tensions rising if results did not go their way during the season.

Despite raising this a number of times, it got lost in the busyness of the preparations for the season. Whilst the campaign started well, the team later went through a losing streak of several games which pushed them out of playoff contention. During this adversity, splits within the coaching team appeared. The head coach became physically and socially more isolated, shifting his style from a consultative one to micromanaging.

Other coaches were left confused and frustrated. The players picked up on these tensions and began to lose confidence. The team failed to recover their league position and missed the playoffs. This adversity of having a new coaching team was predictable but we had failed to address it in the visioning for the season. That was a mistake not to be repeated. The following season, the coaching team went to an island for a weekend to learn from that experience and vision the next season in depth. That next season, they made the playoffs for the first time in eight years.

This need to have the courage and discipline to preview adversity is reflected in the Stockdale Paradox, as articulated by Jim Collins in his bestselling book *Good to Great*. Admiral James Stockdale, one of the highest-ranking naval officers at the time, was held as a prisoner for over seven years during the Vietnam War. During this horrific experience, Admiral Stockdale was repeatedly tortured but did everything he could to help other prisoners survive, including turning down offers of his own release. Admiral Stockdale found a way to stay alive by balancing the harshness of his situation with optimism. Stockdale explained: 'You must never confuse faith that you will prevail in the end – which you can never afford to lose – with the discipline to confront the most brutal facts of your current reality, whatever they might be.'

One historic example of this stands out for me.

On 15 April 1947 Jackie Robinson became the first black player to appear in major league baseball when he took the field for the Brooklyn Dodgers. Over the course of the following decade Robinson would become a Hall of Fame player, World Series winner and become hugely respected for the dignity with which he dealt with blatant racism both on and off the diamond.

Despite his naturally fiery temperament, Robinson showed uncommon self-restraint, particularly in those most intense early years in the league. It has been speculated that the fortitude he generated against racist taunts and indignities came at a high cost to his health, contributing to his early death.

In order to understand Robinson's response to this extreme

provocation we need to go back two years to 28 August 1945. On this day, before signing a contract with the Dodgers, Robinson met its General Manager, Branch Rickey. The meeting lasted for three hours. At that meeting, Branch Rickey set out the Dodgers' vision for success, which included becoming the first integrated team in the league.

Rickey and Robinson visioned what lay ahead in being the first man to break the colour barrier. Rickey used scenarios of racist provocation on and off the diamond to test Robinson's resolve and prepare him for what lay ahead:

'Suppose I'm a player . . . in the heat of an important ball game.' He drew back as if to charge at Robinson. 'Suppose I collide with you at second base. When I get up, I yell, "You dirty black son of a . . ." What do you do?'[71]

Rickey added other scenarios: a desk clerk at a hotel ('We don't let niggers sleep here'); a waiter in a restaurant ('Didn't you see a sign at the door saying no animals allowed?'); a base runner barrelling into Robinson, deliberately spiking him ('*How do you like that, nigger boy?*'); a racist sportswriter and so on.[72]

Together, over those three hours, they rehearsed their response to such provocation. In biological terms, hardwiring the neural pathways that would help automate Jackie Robinson's response to the adversity that became a relentless living reality.

Satisfied with this visualisation and scenario-playing session, and believing that Jackie Robinson could meet with dignity and self-control the cruel forces that awaited him, Branch Rickey signed Jackie Robinson to a professional contract with the Brooklyn Dodgers. After one season with the minor league

Montreal Royals, Jackie Robinson became the first black player in the major leagues on 15 April 1947.

Branch Rickey and Jackie Robinson are our ancestors. They, like the ancient navigators, have knowledge to share. Like them, without knowing the science of neural pathways, they understood that rehearsing foreseeable adversity would enable a ready-made response and keep them on the path to their shared goals.

This is how our ancestors prepared for epic journeys.

4.6 rewriting destiny

A leader is a dealer in hope.
Napoleon Bonaparte

A coach I've enjoyed working with over the years is Vern Cotter. Vern presents as a stoical rock of granite, but he is a caring man with a deep intuitive feel for what teams need in order to be strong. Vern is widely regarded as one of the best coaches in world rugby.

Between 2006 and 2014 Vern coached French club side Clermont Auvergne. He then coached the Scotland national team between 2014 and 2017, ending with that team's highest winning percentage in the professional era. Vern can coach.

With Vern leading Clermont Auvergne the club enjoyed unprecedented success. Prior to his arrival in Clermont the club had never won any title. In Vern's first three seasons with Clermont they made the French final each time and lost each one.

What frustrated Vern even more about those losses was that he sensed the public, and to a degree his team, seemed accepting of the outcome.

Under Vern the club had developed a culture that delivered consistency. They won an almost unbelievable seventy-seven consecutive games at home. But there was something missing when it came to those finals. Vern was confident it was not to do with talent or tactics. It was about the mindset of the collective. There was something in their psyche he did not comprehend. After that third final loss, Vern made it his mission to find out what it was.

In order to more deeply understand this mindset, Vern made contact with a history professor at the local university. They sat down together, shared an espresso and talked. The professor explained to Vern that the town's own identity story was critically shaped by events around 50BC. At this time, Vercingetorix was a chieftain of a Gaul tribe local to Clermont. Vercingetorix led an alliance of tribes in a revolt against the Roman invaders. He won the Battle of Gergovia against Julius Caesar's Roman legions in which several thousand Romans were killed and the legions withdrew. However, in a subsequent battle, Caesar defeated Vercingetorix only after he personally led the last reserves into battle.

The professor explained to Vern that according to legend, in surrendering to Caesar, Vercingetorix dismounted his famous horse in front of the emperor, took off his armour and threw his shield (*bouclier*) before him.

Vercingetorix was taken prisoner and subsequently transported to Rome where he was killed.

The professor explained to Vern that this event had had a profound influence on the sense of identity of the people of this region of France and that Vercingetorix remained a powerful folk hero. Then he shared the breakthrough insight Vern had been seeking. The professor said that Vercingetorix represented the idea of a courageous loser in history. That his destiny was not to prevail, nor to win, but to lose after fighting gallantly.

In the people of the town, this had contributed to an anxiety and superstition when rugby finals arrived. 'Instead of optimism and expectation, there was a sense of gloom and doom. They were more scared of losing than trying to win,' Vern told me. That anxiety was exacerbated the first time Vern lost a final during his reign, where the team led the whole match only to lose it in the last few moments. There was a resignation among many that this was their 'fate'.

Vern set about rewriting the history of the club and the region. He used visioning for the next season to unlock this.

With the professor's insight in hand, Vern found a local blacksmith. He showed the blacksmith a copy of a famous painting of Vercingetorix and his shield and sword at Caesar's feet. Vern instructed the blacksmith to mould and make a replica of the sword. Within a few weeks, the sword was ready. During the off season, Vern had the sword hung down at the reception to the club's training facility.

When the players resumed training Vern gathered them around the sword. He told them the story of Vercingetorix and then laid out his vision for the forthcoming season. Vern pointed to the sword hanging from the ceiling and said that they had recovered Vercingetorix's sword. He said the team now had to go out on a quest to recover the shield (*bouclier*) with it, the *Bouclier* being the name of the French rugby championship.

As part of this new vision, that involved rewriting a tribe's perceived destiny, a ritual was introduced. After each training session, as the players passed the hanging sword on their way home, they would take a stone and sharpen its blade. This became a team mantra of 'sharpening the sword'.

A new mission was set and a different mindset established. To 'sharpen the sword' meant to focus on controllables. The sword and the ritual became an emblem for a growth mindset and constant day-to-day improvement.

That season, for the fourth consecutive year, Clermont made the final again. An unprecedented achievement. This time they won the final, their first title ever. Vern reflects:

'Not many teams would come back from the disappointment of three lost finals, and forty-four months of working and living together, to go again and make history and win the fourth. It showed great character. You can't measure these things, but I think that changing our vision of what was possible was critical to our success.'

169

4.7 the guardian

A vision needs a guardian to protect and nurture it through to fulfilment.

On great voyages, there will be times when doubt will creep in and people, both inside and outside the vessel, may apply pressure to change direction or even abandon the mission.

In order for a vision to survive and be realised it needs a stubborn guardian. Their commitment reinforced by seeing the vision as an expression of the tribe's higher purpose. They understand that people work best when aligned to the same mental pictures of success.

One of those stubborn guardian leaders is my friend Tim Brown, co-founder and co-CEO of Allbirds, a sustainable footwear company based in San Francisco.

In just three years Tim, together with co-founder Joey Zwillinger, has built a business reportedly valued at one and a half billion dollars and had *Time Magazine* name their shoes the most comfortable in the world.[73]

I first met Tim in Tokyo in 2014 when I was asked to do some work with a professional football team he played in. We reconnected the following year when Tim retired from professional sport to undertake a master's degree in management at the London School of Economics. Tim had previously completed a design degree, through a sports scholarship, at the University of Cincinnati.

Whilst meeting up over a coffee or beer Tim would share with me this burning idea that he was carrying with him. His vision was to create a new footwear category where every element of the shoe came from natural materials and was manufactured by sustainable methods.

At that point, the detail of the journey was far from clear. However, a powerful high-level vision was there to work towards.

The vision had originally formed out of Tim's design ideas, particularly his attraction to minimalism and challenging mindless conformity. He would habitually pick off logos from his clothing, even those that sponsored him.

From there, the vision built out as Tim was exposed to the brutal realities of the materials that shoes were made from and how they were manufactured. At the end of one season, Tim visited a shoe manufacturer in Indonesia to see for himself.

Sustainability moved to the centre of Tim's vision, and with it a focus on changing consumer choice and behaviour. Merino sheep wool would become a core material. Tim visualised consumers of the future being increasingly asked to choose between products which would sustain the planet's ecosystem and those that would further damage it. At the centre of this choice was where he saw his shoes.

Every time I met with Tim during this period, I could see the vision becoming clearer. However, he never once mentioned to me any financial ambition or corporate metric. As with the Polynesian voyaging ancestors, the details would reveal themselves as the journey played out. Tim puts it this way:

'Allbirds never set out to build a billion-dollar brand or employ hundreds of people. We wanted to use design and storytelling to become part of a movement around sustainability.'

In those years, the path was far from clear for Tim. In 2016, after graduating from LSE, Tim focused full time on unlocking his business idea. He received an enterprise grant from the Government that allowed him to employ two colleagues. Whilst the prototype design evolved some four hundred iterations, sourcing an investor led down many blind alleys. By year's end the grant had been exhausted, no investor had been found and Tim had to let his two employees go.

The mission in those times was to survive; to cradle the dream until it could sustain its own life. The vision was kept alive by public fundraising and private savings but they, like the Government grant, ran out. Those days were not easy, Tim recalls:

'I would find myself at dinners with friends who were at the stage of their careers where things were starting to take off. We'd go around the table and I'd dread when it would come to me and people would ask what I was doing. My body would curl up in a little ball and I would say, "wool shoes". When we'd leave dinner people would say, "It's lovely that your pursuing this little thing – good luck with that." It was awful.'[74]

What soon became apparent was that the path lay on the other side of the Atlantic Ocean. After considering an offer from a New York-based brand, Tim reconnected with Joey Zwillinger and explored an alternative way of bringing the vision to life. In those conversations, Joey brought another dimension to the Allbirds vision, as Tim explains:

'Joey was on a different path. He felt an urgency because he believed the world was changing and the need to act was now. This was the frustration behind his purpose. He saw that in footwear we had an opportunity to go first.'

Together, they launched Allbirds on 1 March 2016.

In the summer of 2016, Tim and Joey consolidated their shared vision into a two-page document that still guides the company. That vision document has subsequently been shared with, and bought into, by new partners who have come on board such as Leonardo Di Caprio, the San Francisco 49ers and former Starbucks CEO Howard Schultz.

Having watched the journey up close, my respect is deep for the Allbirds story, which has really just begun. As Tim says:

'There were a lot of different off-ramps along the journey where, if you were logical and rational, you would have stopped, and for whatever reason, we've kept going.'

That is the type of guardian a vision needs.

Someone Tim and I both respect is double World Cup-winning All Blacks captain Richie McCaw. Like Tim, Richie is another navigator leader and guardian who sees a vision through to its fulfilment. I once heard Richie use an analogy in how you pursue a vision. He likened it to having a little toy trophy that you'd put in the glovebox in your car. It would be put away from view as you focused your attention on the process of driving the car and navigating the road before you. However, inevitably you'd need to stop, for fuel or rest, and in those times, you might open the glovebox, pull out the little trophy and hold it in your hands. By doing this, you would reconnect to the vision and refuel emotionally. Then, when you were ready to resume the journey, you'd put the little trophy back in the glovebox and drive off, focusing again on the detail.

This is what great guardians do.

5

the silent dance

So that in the first place, I put for a general inclination of all mankind a perpetual and restless desire of power.
Thomas Hobbes, *Leviathan* (1651)

5.1 state of nature

What happens when our ancestors' wisdom set out in the preceding chapters is unheeded?

What takes hold of a group?

Without the guide rails of a strong culture, natural patterns inevitably play out in groups and teams.

Individuals seek security in cliques. Alliances and antagonism surface. Alphas emerge to compete for status and dominance. Cliques and individuals enter into a struggle for influence. Hierarchy, status and opportunity is determined based on the outcome of this struggle.

The group's ways, and how it sees the world, will mirror those of the dominant clique. The group becomes colonised.

Those who came before us feared these primal dynamics of human nature. They worked hard to weave the people together, not allowing the 'laws of the jungle' to reign. They understood that instead of the oneness of *whakapapa* a state of nature would lead to division and weakness. It was also destined to repeat itself periodically as power shifted, sapping the energy and focus of the tribe.

In the 1800s a large-scale state of nature played out in my own country – a group of people thrown together without sharing an identity, purpose or vision.

The indigenous people had been on the land for eight hundred years, organised by family and tribal affiliations. Then traders, whalers, sealers and settlers came. English, Scottish, Irish, Welsh, French, Americans, Germans, Dalmatians, Chinese. Each clique subdivided into further cliques. Factions and differences in the old world reproduced in the new. Among these people thrown together were three lines of my ancestors.

This struggle would end with a new order imposed by the victors. My white ancestors would ascend in influence and status. My brown ancestors would descend in both.

The British, but more specifically the English within that clique, prevailed in this struggle. Their world view became the blueprint for the new nation and took a legal and psychological hold on the people. A treaty was signed that portrayed an equality that did not reflect how power would in reality be exercised.

The new order valued conformity over belonging.

The missionaries arrived and told my grandmother five generations ago, Pakinui, that she was living a sinful life. They told her that there was only one god and that she had been wrong to believe in many male and female gods. They told her that her beliefs in spiritual and herbal healing were mistaken and offended the one god. They told her that traditional marriages were without meaning unless sanctified in a church. They told her of a place called Hell.

The missionaries told Pakinui that the wild stories of her ancestors' feats, such as navigating the Pacific Ocean with purpose and skill, were untrue. Stories that had been preserved for centuries in memory and ritual were superseded by the words of one book.

The missionaries explained to Pakinui that her people's emotional response to suffering lacked dignity and must be replaced by an Anglo-Saxon veiling of such emotion.

On Christmas Eve 1843, nineteen-year-old Pakinui, along with forty others, was baptised by the visiting Wesleyan Reverend James Watkin. Those souls included her two infant sons, Tomati Paraune and Tepene, fathered by visiting whalers when Pakinui was fifteen and then seventeen.

Pakinui was commanded to renounce her ancestors' spiritual ideas and transfer her deepest loyalty from her tribe to the Church authority.

Reverend Watkin wrote in his journal that week *May they be baptised with the Holy Ghost and with fire.*[75]

The service took place on a scarred rocky peninsula that lurches into the Pacific Ocean at Karitane. Below them lay a sweeping bay with an estuary that received the 'turning river' that started in ancient hills and carved its way through the land, to this mouth, where stained whaling ships now lay anchored.

Pakinui was reborn that Christmas Eve in 1843. Reverend Watkin christened her and her sons with new names. Her name was now Mary; her infant sons became Thomas and Joseph. They were given surnames. The boys would be taught English by the missionaries and punished if they were heard to speak their own language.

For a time, in that sweeping bay, the tide of Pakinui's ancient ways went out, and a new tide came in.

Where power resided in the new order was most obvious in how the land was treated. Communal sharing and guardianship that had prevailed for centuries was replaced by private ownership. Through laws, bargains, fraud and confiscations, the land transferred to white settlers.

Pakinui and her people were forbidden from sacred tribal lands and burial grounds. Their timeless rhythm of moving between places with the changing seasons ended. They became shadows across their own land.

Half a world away in the United States, the famed Lakota war chief Sitting Bull, who had defeated General George Custer in the Battle of Little Bighorn, lamented, 'When I was a boy, the Sioux owned the world. The sun rose and set on their land. Where are our lands? Who owns them?'[76]

In 1845 Pakinui married a settler, William Harpur. William, and the eight mixed-race children they would have, were entitled to grants of land that she was not. The land they chose as a family was the same home Pakinui and other survivors had made after fleeing the massacre when she was eight. This had become her true home. Pakinui would live there again until, aged forty-eight, her life ended in the arms of pneumonia. She passed in a time when one in three of her people died from diseases introduced by settlers.

My Irish ancestor, Patrick Daly, was not part of the dominant clique either. In this new order, his Irishness and Catholicism reduced his status. There was more tolerance of his beliefs for they were Christian, but lines were drawn. When the First World War broke out a nephew would refuse to fight for the British and would be harshly punished.

Patrick was denied land that he believed had been promised to him. His challenge in the new courts, set up by the victors, failed. His dream of landholding, that had justified the price of leaving his home and kin, had, in his eyes, been stolen away. Owning land would have to wait at least one more generation. He became embittered. One day he got in a fight in a country hotel. In anger, he cut the strap of his foe's horse so that it ran away. For that, he was arrested, prosecuted and jailed. He now had another label that further lowered his status and opportunities.

He manufactured one concession to this landless plight, though. He had heard that his niece had been forced into an arranged and unhappy marriage in County Kerry. He organised for her to escape to this new country and took care of her. In time, she married into a French settler family with a large land holding in the south.

It was easiest for my English ancestor, Archie Eastwood, who arrived half a century after Pakinui had passed. He would marry her great-granddaughter, my Nana Rose.

Archie belonged to the English clique who had accumulated the most power.

From generations of farm labourers in Sussex, Archie, for having fought in the Great War, was granted free land in this new country. An opportunity was presented that was unimaginable in his 'motherland' where power, status and opportunity were predetermined before he was born.

Archie was gifted land in the 'Bay of Plenty', on the east coast of the North Island. That land had for centuries been the traditional home of descendants of four canoes in the great fleet that had come from Hawaiki. It was also the coastline where the *Takitimu*, which carried my own ancestors, first landed. Archie set to work burning and clearing the wild scrub and bush to make his farm. My father, Māori and English made into one, was born there.

Masses of new migrants, like Patrick and Archie, arrived to transform themselves and the land. Livestock, ploughs and saw-mills came. Rivers were damned. Coal exhumed. Unimagined wealth taken from gold in the rivers. Old tribal trails of one people covered by the roads and railway tracks of another. They brought with them the Industrial Revolution and its brutal efficiency. The concept of work was rewritten – the people were set up to compete with each other now, success measured by monetary value.

Many of the new ways had merit in them. There was progress in there. But it was imposed and rigid. It was one view. No space was made to see what a shared path might look like.

Within the new order, my English ancestor took his place towards the top, my Irish ancestors below, my Māori ancestors at the bottom, along with the Chinese who had come with their own customs that they also refused to surrender. A hierarchy that became a type of caste system.

The weakness was where we knew it would be – the people had not been woven together. Instead, the laws of the jungle had been unleashed. The new tribe was comprised of winners and losers.

After all the chaos and trauma the people still did not have a shared identity, purpose or vision.

Instead, generations inherited misalignment and weakened trust. Energy was diverted away from collective achievement to bandage ongoing grievances and suffering.

These patterns are all around us when *homo sapiens* are thrown together. Communities, groups and teams are weak at their centre when they are colonised by a dominant clique instead of finding a common way.

Philosophers have long debated our fate in its natural state.

To some, such as Thomas Hobbes, we are essentially selfish and prone to use force to get our way. In the *Leviathan*, Hobbes referred to this state of nature as *solitary, poor, nasty, brutish, and short.*[77] This is a theme familiar in fiction, such as in the novel *Lord of the Flies* by William Golding.

Other philosophers have a more charitable view of our natural state. John Locke and Jean-Jacques Rousseau believed that people do not naturally tend to violence against each other but are attracted to reason and natural laws of living co-operatively. This view has recently been refreshed by Rutger Bregman in *Humankind*.

Research over recent decades has now enabled us to see the real dynamics that play out in teams.

This is what I call the 'silent dance'.

5.2 cliques

In our burning need to belong, to feel secure in a potentially intimidating environment, our reflex is to seek out others and form cliques. This is a phenomenon across the animal world known as *homophily*. Professor Robin Dunbar explains:

> 'Cliques are completely normal. We gravitate to people like us. The flow of conversation is easier. We share a similar mental model of the world.'

We look first for shared identity traits in others, such as gender or race, but at the same time we map out potential alliances that may give us most protection and standing. This can lead to less obvious cliques and alliances forming around what we perceive as similar status, experiences or educational backgrounds.[78] It is all about context – whatever best advances our quest for security and advancement.

Cliques are natural and not in themselves good or bad. Their potential harm depends on the wider dynamics.

If there is weakness in the wider culture, then the risk with cliques is that they further fragment the team and distort its work. That each clique develops, maybe unconsciously, its own goals that dilute overall cohesion.

The more time cliques spend with each other, the more they

bond through endorphin-releasing experiences like socialising, laughter and storytelling. This time and emotional investment comes at the cost of building relationships and trust with members of the wider team.

The team can then become a coalition of sub-tribes, with individuals having greater loyalty to their clique than the wider team.

Not long ago, I was invited into a leading football club in Europe. The team was at the time languishing in the middle of its domestic league despite having the highest payroll. It had been underperforming for many months, failing to consistently execute the team's game plan with a number of star players a shadow of their former selves.

When I came into the environment, what was obvious was that the team had divided itself into four cliques, based mainly on nationality. This played out in the canteen, in team meetings, in the placement of lockers in the dressing room, when socialising with families outside the club, and in native languages spoken in communal spaces.

The two most powerful cliques were led by alphas striving to be top dog in the team. One of the two had been appointed captain. This had consolidated his clique as the dominant one. The team culture, the way things were done, largely mirrored their world view.

The competing clique was not on board. They believed the team would have more success if it was made in their image. They became a sub-tribe with their own code. They silently reserved their right to what they did and didn't buy into. Their alpha leader had become disruptive to the point of refusing to follow certain tactical direction.

A third clique, also based on national origin, were the outsiders. They accepted their low status at the club and that they had little chance of influencing the environment. Their purpose was mainly to emotionally support each other.

The final clique was a group of individuals unaffiliated to the others – the 'strays'. In this group was a young star player who had recently joined the team. He shared with me:

'Everyone was quiet in meetings but there was so much activity in these cliques the rest of the time. It was just stressful and distracting. No wonder we played so poorly.'

These dynamics played out in the absence of a unifying culture. There had been no investment in building an Us story (Chapter 2), shared purpose (Chapter 3) or collective vision (Chapter 4). The environment had been set up to accumulate talent and embed a technical and tactical process to win.

What was also missing was an awareness within the leadership of the dynamics that were present in the team. The bigger picture was being missed and instead individuals were superficially being labelled as 'good' and 'bad' guys.

What was needed to move forward was an understanding that the weak cultural architecture at the club was leading to energy-wasting internal competition between cliques and a dysfunctional way of working.

From this low period, work began on clearly and simply articulating the club's purpose, developing an inclusive Us story (including shared values that everyone could attach personal meaning to) and a shared vision for the seasons ahead.

As we have seen, often in groups and teams the status quo is, in truth, a dominant clique's version of the world. Think beyond sport to government, bureaucracy, banking, law firms, educational institutions. Despite the passing centuries, so much of what they do and how they do it mirror how they were set up and by whom. The system is structured to preserve the status quo. The DNA keeps replicating itself.

In Chapter 1 we followed the story of the All Blacks and how they recognised the changing demographics of their team and sought to proactively transform the culture from a traditional Anglo-Saxon approach to an authentically more inclusive one.

I have worked with other leaders who have sought to similarly disrupt how one clique's world view has colonised their organisation.

Those leaders haven't relied on policies or committees or consultants. They have met directly with the diversity of their people and acknowledged that the inherited culture has been disproportionately influenced by one world view. This straightforward acknowledgement is powerful to unlock proper conversations. They then ask their people, *How does the way we do things here work for you? What changes would you make to unlock your full potential?*

Fascinating answers come back that can become rich insights for reimagining a more inclusive culture and working experience:

Something is lost when our work and our goals are translated into dry project plans, spreadsheets and KPIs.

Why does our talent have to be measured every day to the second decimal point?

The way we are appraised is so cold, it lacks humanity.

They say we are to challenge managers but that is not the way

I was raised, and I don't know how to do that. I find it hard to understand our obsession with avoiding mistakes rather than going for it.

From such conversations emerge a re-imagined way of working that authentically reflects the diversity of a team. In my experience, it does not take long to find common ground.

5.3 the status shuffle

As a species, we are obsessed with status.

As Robert Sapolsky puts it:

We're just like numerous other social species in terms of having marked differences among individuals and hierarchies that emerge from those differences. Like many of these other species, we're fantastically attuned to status differences ... and can perceive differences in a blink of an eye.[79]

In fact, within 150 milliseconds of seeing another person we process their social status.[80]

When we join a group, we unconsciously calibrate whether others are higher or lower status than us. We create a status ladder and dominance hierarchy in our minds. On this, we locate ourselves.

A study of three-person groups, unknown to each other, showed that 50 per cent established a clear hierarchy within one minute and all of the groups established a clear hierarchy within five minutes.[81] Another study demonstrated how group members are able to accurately forecast their own future status in a new group by merely viewing others without any words being spoken.[82] Research shows that children as young as three perceive dominance hierarchies and adapt their behaviour accordingly.[83]

We may be quite deferential to those perceived as being above us, though we may also enjoy misfortunes that they may endure.[84] For those below us, we, unfortunately, often aggressively displace our angst on them.[85]

How we map status in teams is based on a complex matrix of factors, including: formal role, clique affiliations, remuneration, external profile, past experience, longevity and proximity to the leader.

Our obsession with status is driven by two primal evolutionary forces. First, a remnant of evolved primate mating habits (where higher status gave access to more reproductive opportunity). We will meet the alphas shortly. Second, the more status we have in a group, the more secure we feel and the less anxiety we experience.

The link between status and wellbeing is increasingly being understood. In *Us and Them*, David Berreby summarises the research in this way:

> . . . *people who think they're low in status are much more likely to suffer stress-related health problems . . . And it turns out that people's perception of their status, not poverty or lack of education, is the important element.*[86]

A key aspect of status is that although we perceive our own position, it is the group that ultimately determines it. The mechanism that this is administered through is our reputation. Our reputation is central to our sense of identity and prospects in a group.

It is, therefore, what others think of us that gives us our ranking. Our self-esteem is directly correlated to this.

In turn, it is gossip that plays a critical role in shaping our reputation. University of Berkeley Professor Dacher Keltner puts it this way in *The Power Paradox*:

Social penalties like gossip, shaming, and ostracism are painful indeed and can easily be misused. But they are also powerful social practices, seen in all cultures, by which group members elevate the standing of those who advance the greater good and prevent those less committed to it from gaining power.[87]

Gossip evolved to constantly check that others were living by our tribal rules. If they were not, then this was a threat to group cohesion. Violations went to the heart of someone's trustworthiness and needed to be identified and publicised. Punishment was principally the experience of shaming and loss of standing in the group. If the violations were severe enough, then more formal steps existed where belonging could be lost through banishment.

People policed themselves. Media and social media fulfil a similar role today in how they monitor the behaviour of higher-status individuals (such as celebrities and politicians), constantly probing for any violations of the tribe's moral code.

The more we promote the group, the higher our status, whilst the less we do for the group (and the more we are perceived as doing for ourselves), our reputation lowers.

A strong reputation generates influence, and therefore power. Dacher Keltner states, *Reputations are amplifiers of the capacity to influence.*[88]

Our dopamine and serotonin systems drive our pursuit of higher status.[89] When we sense our reputation and status has lowered in a group, we feel significant stress, shame and often anger.

Studies of modern social groups concur that most prestige is acquired by individuals that display a high-level mix of both competence and selfless commitment to the group.[90] As Robin Dunbar put it to me:

'You have to perform to have high status in the team. That will cause as much anxiety as anything else.'

Our ancestors understood this. *Mana* (explored in Chapter 3) determines your status, and that of the groups you belong to, based on deeds that unequivocally promote the interests of the tribe. That is non-negotiable. Harm or undermine the collective good and you will lose status no matter what your individual accomplishments.

It is in these ways that our ancestors were able to align our personal quest for status to the wellbeing of the tribe.

Given the proliferation of increasingly individualistic societies in the twenty-first century, this remains one of the critical challenges for leaders of teams today.

5.4 meet the alphas

Alpha males and females are internally driven to acquire top status in a group or team. They want to be, and be seen as, the 'top dog'. They may sense their own hyper competitiveness and focus, but may not be conscious of this ancient remnant of our evolutionary story and general phenomenon in the animal kingdom.

This does not necessarily mean alphas always want to be the formal leader – the status markers they may be more motivated by could be remuneration, internal deference or external recognition as the 'star'.

Not surprisingly, alphas tend to congregate in high-profile and high-reward activities such as elite sport, white-collar professions and politics.

Alphas can bring significant benefits to teams as well as risks. They often bring an intensity and competitiveness than can raise standards in a team. The risk is that their personal desire for status leads them into behaviours that undermine the team dynamic.

Management of alphas is a critical skill in a leader's toolkit.

One of the most high-profile alpha leaders was Michael Jordan, the captain and superstar of the Chicago Bulls team who won six NBA championships in the 1990s. An aspect of the Bulls' success, somewhat underplayed in the 2020 Netflix series *The Last Dance*, was coach Phil Jackson's skill in simultaneously allowing Jordan to feel 'top dog' but also keeping his ego in check. In Jackson's words:

> *The conventional wisdom is that the team was primarily a one-man show – Michael Jordan and the Jordanaires. But the real reason the Bulls won NBA championships . . . was that we plugged in the power of oneness instead of the power of one man, and transcended the divisive forces of the ego . . .*[91]

In the years before the Bulls' first championship Jordan had been the league's leading scorer and wealthiest superstar. He was top dog in the whole of the NBA. He did what he wanted with the ball. When the game was on the line, he took control and the others moved out of his way. However, his team couldn't win a championship.

A key measure undertaken by Phil Jackson was to introduce a game plan, 'the triangle offence', that involved all players and didn't overemphasise the alpha Jordan. No longer would the ball just be put in Jordan's hands and others step aside. Jordan's acceptance of this egalitarian style of play sent a strong message of selflessness to the team and, in turn, enhanced trust and connection. Famously, in the last seconds of critical NBA finals games Jordan did not take the 'glory shot' but instead passed to teammates in better positions who converted and gained their own eternal fame.

Phil Jackson's approach to managing Jordan reflected his own belief in our ancestors' wisdom:

A [Lakota] warrior didn't try to stand out from his fellow band members; he strove to act bravely and honourably, to help the group in any way he could to accomplish its mission.[92]

It takes deep focus by a leader to manage an alpha like Michael Jordan, allowing them a sense of dominance while at the same time having them buy into 'team first' behaviours.

Alphas are often allied with betas who are not personally seeking 'top dog' status but seek influence (power) through their access to leaders. Betas often act as second-in-command to a leader and may step in when the leader departs. Betas typically experience less stress than both the top and bottom of the hierarchy.[93]

There are also, of course, the majority who have no drive or desire to lead or even exert influence. They are comfortable with staying safe and secure in the pack.

In a team I've worked with, we've referred to the alphas as the 'lions', the betas as the 'wolves' and the rest as the 'sheep'. The lions were those individuals who had the competitiveness and confidence to change the game. The wolves would generally stand back and wait on the lions to put the team in the ascendency and then, with the pressure reduced, show their talent and receive acclaim. The sheep's mindset was less about making a real difference and more about just doing what was necessary to retain their place.

There are important gender differences that play out with alphas. Male alphas are more prone to promoting their own achievements and ascending to formal leadership positions in order to display status.[94] Female alphas are less concerned with titles and more on influencing the group.

Sometimes a team dynamic is more settled where there are two or three clear alphas. The reason being that when a clear hierarchy is quickly formed within a group, it is able to settle down and better focus on the task at hand. In contrast, where hierarchy and status are unclear and confused and continually shifting, then the team can become distracted by political manoeuvrings and become dysfunctional as internal order falls apart.

Ideally, the alphas marry their internal drive with a selfless commitment to the group – like Michael Jordan. Life will often not be that blessed. Alphas can be ego-driven and selfish. Their obsession with internal competition and dominance detracts from the work and creates chaos.

How leaders manage alphas in these situations can be critical to whether a team succeeds or becomes dysfunctional. In reality, treatment of alphas is often tied to their perceived talent value. If they are a world-class performer, egotistical behaviours are more likely to be tolerated. There are many examples where such alphas are made leaders in order to keep them on side. However, they are ill equipped to lead others and the team suffers as a result.

How an alpha is managed will have repercussions in their clique within the team. If an alpha is removed or socially shamed, this can raise tensions and reinforce divisions among cliques.

There is nearly always an option between appointment as leader and banishment. It may involve dispensing high status in creative ways, such as appointing them to a leadership team, encouraging them to mentor young talent, giving them a special advisory role or engaging them in high-profile media commitments.

As with cliques themselves, the impact of alphas will ultimately be determined by the strength of the culture they are in.

5.5 the leader we want

A leader is best when people barely know he exists, when his work is done, his aim fulfilled, they will say: we did it ourselves.

Lao Tzu

In primates, leadership of small groups requires the consent of the team to be effective and sustainable. Studies by Dacher Keltner's team at Berkeley have found:

Whereas the Machiavellian approach to power assumes that individuals grab it through coercive force, strategic deception, and the undermining of others, the science finds that power is not grabbed but is given to individuals by groups.[95]

Whilst in teams today we may not always get a direct say in who the leader is, these evolved preferences persist. This means that the success of a leader is heavily reliant on 'buy in' by the team. This insight continuously plays out in sport (a coach's tenure often ends after they are seen to have 'lost the dressing room').

Our desire for protection and stability leads to a preference in smaller groups for composed selfless leaders over ego-driven bullying leaders. The idea of 'servant leadership' is far from an enlightened new model – it is our ancient way.

In groups of around 150 or fewer (known as 'Dunbar's number' after groundbreaking research by Professor Robin Dunbar and his team at Oxford University) relations are largely face to face and personal.

In these smaller groups our need to belong and feel safe are acute. The dynamics in the group are intimate and visceral. It is in these smaller groups that we have spent the vast majority of our existence as a species.

We have an aversion to conflict and prefer leaders who can find non-extreme solutions when tensions arise. Our anxiety levels are reduced when we know our leaders will put the interests of the group before their own, and they will not needlessly put us at risk through their recklessness or belligerence. As Robin Dunbar put it to me:

'We look for "wise" people as leaders who can calm situations down and find some form of solution, so outcomes feel equitable and people are not left aggrieved.'

Dacher Keltner says:

Groups demonstrate an instinctive tendency to give power to individuals who bring the greatest benefit and least harm to individuals.[96]

As part of this preference, *homo sapiens* seek humility in their leaders. This is seen today in traditional collectivist societies and modern hunter-gatherer bands. One such living example is the !Kung who have a ritual called 'shaming the meat':

'. . . when a young man kills much meat he comes to think of himself as a chief or a big man, and he thinks of the rest of us as his servants or inferiors. We can't accept this. We refuse one who boasts, for some day his pride will make him kill somebody. So we always speak of his meat as worthless. This way we cool his heart and make him gentle.'[97]

This same evolved preference is articulated by the Native American Indian Lakota people. The *wapaha*, the eagle-feathered headdress worn by their chiefs, symbolises acting on behalf of the people. Eagle feathers would be given for selfless acts, from an act of generosity to success on the battlefield. As Lakota elder Duane Hollow Horn Bear explains:

'The individual who wears the eagle-feather headdress has earned prestige and accepted responsibility and portrays these in a very humble way.'[98]

Humility strongly signals that 'the group is more important than me'. A humble leader is perceived as prioritising the well-being of others. They cause us less anxiety.

Herein we can see the role of self-deprecating behaviours. We are signalling that we put others before ourselves; that we can be trusted.

This may sound remote from leadership today. Not so. In Jim Collins' management classic *Good to Great* he profiled exceptional leadership based on deep research of sustained successful companies. Collins and his research team called these elite leaders the 'Level 5 Executive'. The defining feature of these leaders is *a paradoxical blend of personal humility and professional will.*[99] Collins details:

In contrast to the very I-centric style of comparison leaders, we were struck by how the good-to-great leaders didn't talk about themselves. During interviews with the good-to-great leaders, they'd talk about the company and the contributions of other executives as long as we'd like but would deflect discussion about their own contributions. When pressed to talk about themselves they'd say things like, 'I hope I'm not sounding like a big shot.'[100]

Words such as 'humble', 'modest', 'self-effacing' and 'understated' were used by colleagues of these Level 5 leaders.[101]

The same could be said of the leader of a hunter-gatherer tribe sixty thousand years ago.

So, why do we often get the opposite in teams today? Leaders prone to be ego-driven and even bullying in their style – the opposite of the preferences we have evolved over millennia?

One reason is that our model today of a good leader has become contaminated. Leaders and managers of small teams mimic styles they see in large-scale groups (like corporations and nations). As Robin Dunbar puts it:

'Our leaders come from our wider society. They bring in a conception of leadership they've learned from these large-scale societies which may have thuggish attitudes at the top. Smaller groups are much more democratic in nature than that.'

This misplaced model of leadership is exacerbated by portrayals of leaders on screen and the antics of coaches on sidelines.

In groups of more than 150 people the relationship between leader and tribe members is generally neither personal nor intimate. Instead, rules, formality and institutions have been constructed to manage people.

Leaders of large-scale communities need different traits and skills to attain and maintain power. We have evolved a higher tolerance for more egocentric and even bullying leaders in these large-scale groups. Personal ambition is often accepted as their motivation. In smaller tribes, this has never been our model of a leader.

5.6 the backstory

On 2 November 2019, South Africa won their third Rugby World Cup in Yokohama, Japan. The team was captained by Siya Kolisi, the team's first black captain in its 126-year history.

The team won acclaim around the world for the inclusive culture its success had been built upon. Siya had signalled this evolution well before the World Cup:

> 'I tell my teammates that you should never play just to represent one group. You can't play to be the best black player or to be the best white player to appeal to a community; you have to play to be the best for every South African.'[102]

As with most epic achievements, there is a long backstory.

Arriving at this place, admired not just for their play but for their progressive attitudes and environment, did not come quickly or easily for the Springboks.

Alongside historic poor results in recent years, there was a long-standing sense that the team underperformed with arguably the best talent in the world.

I gained my own impression of the Springboks' internal struggles in 1981 when I had just turned thirteen, the same year I received my belonging letter from my tribe *Ngāi Tahu*.

The Springboks toured New Zealand in 1981 despite significant opposition at home and criticism internationally. Intense protests took place outside match venues, resulting in violent clashes with police. Such scenes deeply shocked our country.

On the winter weekends of 1981 I was a ball boy for our local provincial rugby team Southland. On Saturday 8 August 1981 the Springboks played us. As a precaution for this match the ball boys were replaced by police officers. We were disappointed not to be on the grass with the players, but we understood. As compensation, we were given prime seats in the main stand to watch the match that day.

After the full-time whistle had blown an official walked over and invited us into the Springboks' dressing room to meet the players. When I got to the dressing room door one of the iconic Springboks, Naas Botha, came over, smiled and shook my hand. He led us into that sacred space and took us around to meet some of the muddied and bloodied players about to shower.

Botha looked at me and asked whether there was any particular player I wanted to meet. I awkwardly replied, 'Errol Tobias.' I loved the attacking style of play he had shown on the tour. Tobias had also, the previous year, become the first black player ever selected for the Springboks. He was seated alone in his blazer and tie on one of the benches along the dressing room wall. Botha took me over to him and introduced me. I sat with Tobias for a short time. That poignant image of him sitting there alone in his blazer never left me.

Decades later I would form a great friendship with a former Springboks captain Bob Skinstad. Bob played for the Springboks over an eleven-year period, captaining the team twelve times. Bob debuted just two years after the team's iconic 1995 World Cup win, when Nelson Mandela, wearing his own Springboks shirt, handed over the trophy to Francois Pienaar. By the time Bob retired he had his own World Cup winner's medal from his last year in the team, 2007.

That success in 2007 was followed by the team's worst results in its history until Siya Kolisi and coach Rassie Erasmus joined forces a year before their 2019 World Cup success.

Bob is now a partner in a successful private investment firm. His role involves guiding senior executives in terms of leadership and building high-performing teams. This work has forced him to reflect deeply on his own experiences in the Springboks.

When Bob thinks back to his early years as a Springbok, he describes a team culture that was caught between a traditional white conservative model, established inside the team over a hundred years, and the new world of a transformed nation under the leadership of Nelson Mandela.

Caught between these two worlds, there was an anxiety as to how to change the way things were done without derailing a highly competitive team.

In the end, the status quo kept on replicating itself.

This conservative traditional model was pervasive across all levels of the game at the time. The void created by the absence of a strong inclusive centre, that pulled everyone in, was filled by power held in cliques and hierarchical leadership expressed in a highly directive manner.

Bob first became exposed to this pervasive culture when he came through the youth ranks. As a sixteen-year-old he was selected for the national schools' team, one of only two non-Afrikaner players:

'I really enjoyed that experience. What stood out to me was that the environment was much more conservative and religious than what I was used to. I saw how the coach was a traditional father-like figure, dominating the space, which was a little different to what I was used to.'

This cultural model was reproduced when he went on to attend Stellenbosch University and was then selected in provincial teams. Bob was shockingly reminded of the rules of hierarchy on his first day with the Western Province senior team. Innocuously, Bob put his sports bag down under a random peg in the dressing room. A senior player came straight over to him, punched him and threw his kit across the floor. Humiliated, Bob retreated to the edges of the dressing room. He had inadvertently breached unwritten rules on status and hierarchy within the team and was socially shamed for this infringement.

In November 1997, aged twenty-one, Bob was called up to the Springboks.

He had become familiar with the ever-present cliques within teams as his career had progressed. This was something that he didn't enjoy because of his own highly social personality and unique background. He was not someone easily pigeonholed.

Looking back, Bob identifies the lack of space made in the Springboks to truly get to know each other as a shortcoming that empowered cliques and reduced trust and togetherness:

'I was seen by some as an outsider. It was known I was born in Bulawayo [in Zimbabwe] and I was labelled by some as a lesser form of South African. My name is Norwegian so I didn't naturally fit into any clique.'

Over Bob's eleven-year career with the Springboks only a few ever got to learn his own backstory.

Yes, Bob had been born in Bulawayo in 1976 and moved with his parents to Pietermaritzburg in South Africa in 1981 upon the conclusion of the civil war in Zimbabwe. But his connection to South Africa was much deeper.

Bob's great-grandparents, Niels and Anna Skinstad, had emigrated to South Africa in the 1890s from Norway. Niels had grown up in a working-class family, Anna from a much wealthier social set. They had secretly married.

As a young man Niels had been a passive objector to the war in the country, and after time in prison, exile was his only real option for a new life.

In 1898 Niels boarded a ship from Norway bound for Durban with the express promise to his bride that he would send funds for her to purchase a ticket, and she would then follow. When he arrived in South Africa, Niels used his carpentry skills to raise the money for Anna's ticket. Upon receiving the funds, Anna boarded her ship to sail to Durban and reunite with her loved one.

However, whilst Anna was at sea conflict between the Afrikaans settlers and the colonial British Government broke out, resulting in the Boer War.

Niels started to make his way from Johannesburg to Durban to meet Anna. But because of the war Niels had to follow a circuitous route that took months longer than he had planned. They had no way of directly communicating with each other.

After waiting forlornly for several months in Durban, Anna concluded that Niels must have died on his way – not uncommon in those times, particularly in war. She explained her situation to a priest in Durban who allowed her to join a convent and become a nun.

Eventually, Niels made his way across the scarred baked landscape, escaping capture, and arrived in Durban. There he asked whoever he met about his Norwegian bride. Finally, someone directed him to the convent where she had taken her vows. There, they were at last reunited.

Niels and Anna spent the next few years making their home first in Durban and then north towards Johannesburg. Niels was able to specialise in building church steeples. Six of the churches he built can still be seen today. They have a distinct style as Niels was known for the steepness of his steeples which were based on the Norwegian design that ensured snow would quickly fall away (not a characteristic necessarily suited for South Africa).

Bob's father, Alvin Skinstad, was born in an Afrikaans suburb of Johannesburg and went to Afrikaans schools. He then studied medicine in Pietermaritzburg, near Durban. The medical school had a campus in Harare, Rhodesia (now Zimbabwe). Bob's parents relocated there, and Bob was born in Bulawayo where Alvin worked his first job as a qualified doctor. When civil war broke out Alvin was conscripted and compelled to serve with the Government forces. This is why Bob was born in Zimbabwe and lived there until he was four.

Bob had a deep personal sense of being South African. But in the absence of shared stories in the Springboks, doubt in other minds lingered as he and others had labels attached to them. In Bob's words:

'Unfortunately, the team culture at the time didn't provide the space for personal backgrounds and mutual understanding to emerge and be shared.'

The team's lack of cultural togetherness and the silent role of cliques was dramatically brought into focus the day before Bob's debut match against England in London on 29 November 1997.

As is tradition, the day before the international match the team undertook a light training run at the Twickenham ground (known as the 'Captain's run'). At the end of the light run, the players ritually formed a huddle at the centre of the field.

A senior player, clearly moved, spoke about how, in the game against England the next day, they would be playing in front of thousands of descendants of those who had brutalised their ancestors in concentration camps during the Boer War a hundred years before. That it was their duty to avenge that history and win this match.

This was the world view of the dominant clique in the team but not that of others. In fact, there were many players in that huddle with British ancestry. Bob himself, on his maternal side, had English relations who were coming to watch him play the next day. Whilst Bob had deep empathy for the experiences of the Afrikaners in its war with the British, that was not his Us story as a South African nor that of many of his teammates.

Despite playing his first game for the Springboks, and it being a resounding win over England, the dynamic of the team had an unsettling effect on Bob:

'I had been warned to take care in navigating the environment, that there was complexity and it would not be straightforward. But I'm a child of the sunshine and the smile. They were proved right – I walked right into it.'

The unwritten rules and boundaries of the team were becoming clearer to him. The role of cliques more obvious: who people habitually spent their time with. He noticed that when issues arose in the team he would sometimes be approached by others exploring potential alliances. It was complicated.

The cliques that had naturally formed in the team were paradoxically invisible and in full sight.

There were always a number of alphas in the team. He recalls a respected past player who came back to the team having, what appeared to Bob, a disproportionate impact on the team's direction:

'Although he wasn't the captain or a formal leader it seemed like he was running the ship through force of personality and his status and reputation among the senior players. It was very confusing for a young player to understand.'

As Bob puts it, 'there was no user's manual' to navigate these team dynamics.

There was no induction or welcome or guidance for those transitioning into the team. There was no mentoring of new players nor a forum for them to express themselves. Invisible lines and blind spots were everywhere. The sharpness of these edges was not something within Bob's previous life experience.

By the end of his first season with the Springboks, Bob's father Alvin privately diagnosed him as suffering from a stress-related illness:

'I was exhausted by the energy expended. I'm an empathetic person so could pick up quickly on any negativity or tension or hostility. I felt like I was fighting for survival at every point – always swimming upstream. I just didn't have the wherewithal to understand or navigate the environment I walked into. It's not all about me, a lot of guys suffered and struggled to perform at their best.'

The culture that prevailed in the team had come from another era and was creaking.

On the face of it, this was an outstanding team. The Springboks won thirteen of Bob's first fourteen internationals. While the team kept winning, the fragility of the culture was papered over. The status quo persisted.

However, the team was about to start a gradual slide which would last a decade.

A turning point for this decline was a match they would lose against England a year after Bob's debut. In the intervening time, Bob had moved from being an impact player off the bench to an established starter and star player. However, even then he remained an outsider.

A few days before this match, Bob inadvertently walked into a gathering of his unit in the team. He had not been invited to the meeting.

Bob is now better able to analyse the team dynamics at the time:

'There were good guys across the board, but the interactions were complex, and a lot of behaviours made little sense to me. I can see clearly now that it was part of a maturation process for the Springboks – that all these experiences have contributed to a vision of a more inclusive and progressive culture that the team has today. I'm at peace with that.'

One regret Bob carries is that when he became captain of the Springboks himself, he was not equipped to fully understand these dynamics and disrupt the inherited status quo. Bob reflects:

'In my twenties, my experience and understanding of these forces was at its lowest but my need for it was at its highest.'

One of Bob's abiding memories of his time as captain is speaking in a team huddle in the dressing room before a test match and a clique of players then going off to the back of the dressing room and having their own huddle before they took the field: 'I suppose that symbolised our fragmented culture in those years.'

Bob feels passionately that leaders, particularly inexperienced ones, need external support in understanding team dynamics and developing their own leadership framework. This is what I call 'situational coaching': a focused engagement that accelerates a leader's ability to positively influence their particular environment. This is one of the most satisfying areas of my work today. It is also where Bob now deploys much of his time as an investment partner.

The backstory to the Springboks' recent rise illustrates how the evolution of a team or organisation's culture can be messy, a little crazy and uncomfortable. What they've strikingly demonstrated, though, and our ancestors insisted upon, is that we must learn as we go.

5.7 flattening the hierarchy

Our evolutionary story has hardwired a need for fairness in groups. As Robin Dunbar put it to me:

'Primate groups are really just co-operative ventures. They are a collective attempt to solve life's problems. But there are always tensions around what we've contributed and how we are treated relative to others.'

We do not require equality, but we are finely tuned for fairness in how status and resources are allocated.

This intrinsic pursuit of fairness evolves in us as children. Stanford Professor Robert Sapolsky explained it to me in this way:

'Homo sapiens have absolutely evolved a need for fairness in groups. You can see this transition in kids from (i) I want that; to (ii) that should be shared by me and my friends, but with me getting the most; to (iii) equal sharing; to (iv) emotionally distant meritocratic thinking (Kid A deserves this more than Kid B); to (v) Kid A is more deserving than me and should get more.'

Our sense of fairness is a marker for weighing the pros and cons of being in a group. When we feel exploited, we experience anxiety relating to our belonging and the possibility of being better off elsewhere. When we sense unfairness present, we also become anxious about the strength of the group which, in turn, hormonally impacts on our motivation and bonding with others.

One of the ways this need for fairness plays out in smaller teams is a preference for a flattened hierarchy.

We generally experience more anxiety with a dictator-led venture than in a team where ownership of the mission is shared.

The ideas of distributed leadership and decentralised decision-making have been popularised in recent years, through books such as *Team of Teams* by retired US Army General Stanley McChrystal. However, this is actually our long-evolved preference.

We know that once puberty hits, the greatest influence on young people's behaviour is generally their peers, not authority figures.[103] So, it would be nonsensical not to deploy respected peers to influence their teammates' behaviour.

Today, younger generations grow up less conditioned by hierarchy and want a voice in how the team is run. One of the coaches I've particularly enjoyed working with is England football manager Gareth Southgate. He has developed a coaching philosophy which intentionally flattens hierarchy:

'Back then, football reflected society, where the boss gave the orders, was never challenged and was probably aggressive. And it felt like everybody was afraid to go against them. Players today have a different view of the world. They want to have a say, to be involved in the decision-making, and I love that. We should all be challenged to justify our reasoning and constantly evolve the way we manage people.'[104]

When Vern Cotter became head coach of the Scotland rugby team in 2014, he was also focused on flattening the team's traditional hierarchical approach. This reflected Vern's belief that for the team to become more competitive the players needed to be empowered to lead themselves.

In Vern's first meeting with the team in October 2014 he set out his vision.

At the centre of this vision was a strong player leadership group that he named the 'Thistle Group'.

In this meeting Vern challenged the traditional top-down way teams were set up. He shared his belief that players developed and performed better when they took responsibility as opposed to passively waiting to be told what to do.

Vern described the Thistle Group working in partnership with the coaches and management. He forcefully observed that the team's standards of conditioning, skills and game understanding needed to be dramatically improved and that this would be the immediate priority for the Thistle Group. Vern committed to investing time with the Thistle Group to coach them on how to lead and work as a team in their own right. I assisted Vern and the player leaders in this.

Vern then stepped back and further visioned the three-year project he had embarked upon. He told the team that in Year One he would necessarily take quite a directive approach as coach as he raised standards. He noted that they may not always enjoy his style that first year, but the work would be necessary to help the team to make progress towards real competitiveness. He set out his expectations of the Thistle Group in Year One: that they would be accountable for role-modelling higher standards in the team and driving their teammates to match them.

Vern then visioned that a transition would take place in Year Two where, with the Thistle Group's maturation, they would be expected to share their views with team management on how to improve preparation, training, tactics and the team environment. He made it clear that he expected the coaches' thinking to be challenged.

Finally, Vern visioned that in Year Three he would pass 'ownership' of the team over to the players. He said that when the team would come into camp that season, he would ask the players what they wanted to achieve and what style of game they wanted to play. He would then do his best to facilitate their own vision.

The Thistle Group was not treated as a process measure but as a sacred duty. Through the work of Katie Stevenson at St Andrews University, we shared stories with the player leaders of how in medieval times an Order of the Thistle had been established by the King of Scotland, comprising a group of the twelve best knights in the kingdom who reviewed recent military campaigns and gave their frank opinions to the King.

As well as consulting with, and at times challenging, their coaches, the Thistle Group played both a formal and informal role in managing their peers in terms of commitment and buy-in to the team code. If a player breached that code, it was the Thistle Group who were first responsible for addressing the issue.

The Thistle Group's membership evolved over time as players came and went and new leaders emerged from within the ranks. However, through the full three-year period they were led by captain Greig Laidlaw. Greig reflects this way on the impact of the Thistle Group:

'Many coaches talk about players leading but they never really let them do it. They like to keep control and don't really trust their players. But a team really does run better when the hierarchy is flat and it is self-managed. Vern actually did that, and it was a major reason for our rapid improvement as a team.'

Greig noticed how the Thistle Group took energy away from certain natural cliques that would usually form. The Thistle Group itself was intentionally highly inclusive and accelerated the forming of new relationships.

On 22 January 2017, the start of Year Three, Vern addressed the team when they assembled at the Dalmahoy Hotel outside Edinburgh. He welcomed everyone. He then referred back to his first talk with the team and the journey they had visioned and pursued.

Vern repeated what he had said in that first meeting, that in Year Three the Thistle Group would truly take ownership of the team. He then asked the coaches and management to join him in leaving the meeting room so the players alone could discuss what they wanted to achieve in that Six Nations Championship and how they wanted to do it.

That moment is seared into Greig Laidlaw's memory:

'That was a very powerful moment. We had never been given that type of respect by a coach before.'

The Thistle Group facilitated that discussion among the players. An hour later the team management returned to the meeting room. The Thistle Group set out to the coaches and staff their aspiration for the championship and the way they wanted to play. Vern listened and replied that it was his job to do everything he could to facilitate their own vision.

What followed was Scotland's best ever Six Nations Championship, where the team won all three home games, losing in extra time to France in Paris and being that win away from its first championship in two decades. The team ended the season with a world ranking of fifth, its highest ever, up from tenth when they first met up three years before.

At the heart of this turnaround was a flattening of the hierarchy in the team and a transfer of responsibility and accountability to the players. This became part of the team's new Us story: a return to a sacred Scottish way of shared ownership – an ancient tradition inherited from the Order of the Thistle seven hundred years before.

6

the glue

Let me fall if I must fall.
The one I will become will catch me.
                    The Baal Shem Tov

6.1 sacred spaces

One winter afternoon when I was still at school, my team went through its routine of sitting in the dressing room listening to our coach's final instructions before we took the field. It was a game we would go on to win easily. I always listened attentively to those final instructions. Sometimes, as was the case on this day, as I listened, I translated my nervous energy into fiddling with the laces of my boots. As I did so on this occasion, there was a pause in the coach's speech and then . . . he struck me across the side of my head.

The coach then shouted at me for my perceived lack of attention and continued on with his speech. I went out and played my worst game of the season. We never spoke of this incident.

I don't recall the fleeting physical pain of being struck, but over three decades later the emotional pain has stayed with me. In one moment, the trust that had been built up over countless hours that season was shattered.

I can draw a direct line between that incident and the work I do today, helping leaders build healthy and inspiring performance environments.

Up to that moment in the season I had confidence in how my leader would behave towards me. Although firm, my calculation, based on months of evidence, was that he cared about me and had my best interests at heart. After he struck me, that evaporated. I could no longer predict with confidence his intentions or future behaviour towards me.

Later in the season, we trained in a storm. By the time we had finished it was dark and I had a seven-mile bike ride awaiting me, directly into the lashing rain and biting wind. My coach came across and told me to put my bike in the boot of his car and he drove me home. It was an act of kindness.

However, despite this, the damage to trust had been done. I had lost confidence in predicting how he would act towards me. There was no consistency.

Our team went on to win the competition, and I played well enough, but that moment signalled the end of my improvement that season.

My mindset shifted from expressing myself to avoiding mistakes. Instructions that needed clarifying and opportunities to improve were left hanging as I avoided vulnerability. I could not confidently predict whether any weakness I presented would be met with care or anger. From that moment, emotional energy, better directed towards performing, leaked in an environment that I'd learned could turn hostile in an instant.

Today, we have the language for this: it had become a psychologically unsafe environment.

Many years later I was chatting with my friend Michael Gervais, who among his other roles is the performance psychologist for the Seattle Seahawks NFL team, and he shared with me their team's saying: *years of building a relationship can be ended in seconds*. In that context, this can even be a look of annoyance or anger towards a player's mistake that is shown on the stadium screen and replayed on television afterwards. Such a reaction can seriously damage the trust between player and coach.

A legacy of this experience was the honing of my own trust antenna. I suspect that more than most, I habitually and consciously scan environments for readings on trust.

I later came to learn that corporate environments could be trust minefields. Before working in private practice as a lawyer, I spent two years working in an investment bank. I was part of a small team set up to work out the mechanics underlying new areas of trading.

One day I accompanied my manager to a high-level meeting. There were about thirty of us sitting around a table with the divisional chief in charge. Towards the end of the meeting, the chief directed his attention to my boss and asked him if he agreed that focus should be directed to a particular interest rate swap product. My boss agreed, without hesitation. The chief directed him to put a paper together and circulate it that day. My boss smiled and nodded, and the meeting came to an end.

On our way back to the office I said to my manager, 'I'm really sorry about this but I don't have a clue about interest rate swaps – would you mind explaining them to me before I start on this?'

He replied, 'Don't worry, I don't have a clue what they are either.'

Here was proof of a low-trust, psychologically unsafe environment. The result was my manager recklessly endorsing a financial strategy because he was fearful of the consequences of admitting to his chief and peers that he did not understand the product. His prediction was that something bad would happen to him if he was honest in that moment. He did what he had to do to not risk rejection from this tribe.

It is fair to say that when the global financial crisis happened a few years later, I was probably less surprised than most.

Lack of trust damages tribes.

A thousand years ago, the ancient Polynesian navigators prepared to voyage across the largest ocean in the world. The evening before they departed, they shared food and their Us story around the fire. Remnants of clues exist of how, the evening before those voyages, the navigator asked each person to describe their role to the others. Once this was done, the navigator invited everyone to speak of anything they were unclear about.

Trust was at the centre of that sacred space, binding them together as they set out on their epic mission.

6.2 keeping close together

Waiho i te toipoto, kaua i te toiroa
(Let us keep close together, not far apart)

Māori proverb

Trust is an emotional state reflecting our assessment of whether we can rely on those around us.

We are continually scanning our environment and judging whether it is physically and psychologically safe for us. This adaptive skill evolved to promote our safety by allowing us to predict significant moments ahead and adapt accordingly. From a basic survival tool, we now use this system to assess safety in working with others.

Trust cannot be commanded or willed. It is a deep-seated primal calculation we make on evidence from our environment and how others relate to us. Our hormonal state, particularly our anxiety levels, delivers the answer.

The most learning I have had around trust has come from working with French behavioural psychologist Eric Blondeau:

'Trust is an emotional state, not a rational calculation. We look for evidence in others to alleviate fear and reduce stress.'

Trusting others puts us in an inherently vulnerable position. It is a (calculated) risk. Others may not do what they are supposed to do. They may let us down. They may not have our best interests at heart. We may fail due to them. We may be left in harm's way. However, the alternative is disconnection and dysfunction in working together.

The proof of the importance of trust is the intense emotional pain that accompanies it being broken.

When our sense of trust is high, we are less fearful, less anxious, more confident and optimistic.

When trust is low, we experience a physical stress response. We may be debilitated through stress hormones and adrenalin. Other times, the response will be less severe but will be unhealthy in terms of our connection with others and will prevent us from performing at our best.

Trust is never fixed. It is highly contextual. It is always being calculated and recalculated based on the latest data. We can have high and low levels of trust in the same individual depending on what situation we are in with them. I may have a high level of trust in a lawyer friend relating to an issue with a contract, but low levels of trust five minutes later when we are chatting about problems with my plumbing.

When we deeply trust those around us, we experience a sense of inner peace. Performance psychologist David Galbraith described for me in this way what high trust feels like in a team:

'Everyone is clear on what needs to be done. They are not looking to the sideline for direction or approval. They are locked into each other as they do the work. You can see the team fall into these moments of deep connection. They are being vulnerable but feel safe because of the trust there. There is a feeling of inner peace among them.'

So, what can we do environmentally and relationally to strengthen trust in working with each other?

Eric Blondeau highlights six critical elements as impacting on trust levels in teams. In Eric's words, 'If any of these elements are missing, then fear will increase and trust will decline.'

I don't particularly like checklists but when I'm having conversations with leaders on trust these are what we work through.

AUTHENTICITY

What we say and what we do are the same. At the heart of this is integrity – in terms of honesty and following through on what we undertake to others.

Even before events play out, if we sense a disconnect between what someone says and their body language, our threat detection system is activated. We become anxious and trust reduces.

LOYALTY

That we all live by the tribe's code; that we accept and respect those standards and refuse to break them for our own self-interest. When our tribal identity and code is unclear or there is a tolerance of individuals opting out, then anxiety is higher and trust weakens.

COMPETENCE

That I can do the tasks that have been given to me.

CONSISTENCY

That our behaviour and performance is consistent over time so that it can be confidently predicted by those around us. When someone new comes into a team they are often reassured that they are trusted. However, deep trust has to be accompanied by real evidence and there is no replacement for the shared experience of working together, which takes time.

An interesting study of London stock market traders by John Coates and Joe Herbert of Cambridge University highlights our deep aversion to inconsistency. Their study shows that traders experience greater stress responses to an unpredictable market than they do to a bad market.[105]

Often people who make unilateral decisions on 'gut instinct' are lauded as natural leaders. Whilst I believe we should listen to our gut, I have seen such leaders struggle to engender deep trust in their teams. This is because their decisions are, by definition, hard to predict and not necessarily consistent. That leads to confusion and anxiety, both of which erode trust.

ADAPTABILITY

That in the face of an unknown, complex and chaotic environment we are open-minded and able to change. This is the confidence we have in leaders who can see that Plan A is not working in the current reality and are able to toggle to Plan B.

(EMOTIONAL) AVAILABILITY

In Eric's words, 'when you need me, I'll be there'. The antithesis of emotional availability is abandonment.

This need for emotional availability can be seen when we are children in an uncertain or stressful moment – how we gain a sense of safety from peering at a parent. This crosses into adult life. Our need for protection shifts over time from parents to teachers, to community leaders, to coaches and bosses. We do not suddenly turn this model off when we get paid to perform or work.

The correlation between trust and intimate connection was reinforced to me in a conversation with Yuhui Choe, first soloist at the Royal Ballet Company in London's Covent Garden. I asked Yuhui the question of how trust works with a partner as they perform at the Opera House in front of thousands. She replied:

'You can only dance freely if you know the person is there for you. It is not about words between you. It is in their eyes.

231

There you can see whether they are with you in that moment or their mind is somewhere else.'

This is a powerful insight from Yuhui. *Homo sapiens* have the largest whites of any primates' eyes. This allows us to carefully but unconsciously scrutinise the movement of each other's pupils. As a joint study in 2014 by the University of Virginia and the Max Planck Institute put it:

Human eyes serve two key functions in face-to-face social interactions: they provide cues about a person's emotional state and attentional focus.[106]

This takes us back into our evolutionary story where we knew everyone face to face in our tribe and trust was a very personal commodity.

Stanford Professor Robert Sapolsky emphasised to me that we can be working with someone who is competent and consistent but if we sense a potential underlying hostility or coldness towards us, trust will be compromised.

The Seattle Seahawks' head coach Pete Carroll captures emotional availability in his coaching philosophy like this:

'Call us crazy, but we really believe if you cherish the people in your organization and see them as the unique, extraordinary individuals they are, with all of the special things they offer your environment, and you celebrate that, everything is going to be better. It's really a simple thought, but you do it by loving and caring for the people you have around you.'[107]

Such a relational approach reduces fear and anxiety within a team and increases the conditions for trust.

We have been hardwired over millennia to expect that we can trust those in our kin and in our tribes – groups of people with a shared interest in our wellbeing. When things get tough, we're going to be fairly confident they have our backs.

Our need to trust transcends into other groups we belong to. In these teams where personal connections may not have pre-existed trust becomes more difficult to assume.

Some come into teams having been conditioned through their families and other life experiences to trust others. That's their starting position.

Others are just waiting to be let down. They may have come from difficult home lives or have open wounds from traumatic experiences in groups. They come with high scepticism of what is said and promised; they do not expect words and deeds to be the same thing; they see little sense in being vulnerable or relying on others. They are trigger-happy to write relationships off.

Their working assumption is that this will not be a safe place and they need to stay in self-protection mode. It will take acres of proof from their leaders and teammates to convince them otherwise.

Better leaders make no assumptions about what experiences people come into teams with; they get to know their people and work from there.

Gareth Southgate is a relation-based coach. This approach to being emotionally available to others is something he picked up while observing his father as he grew up:

233

'I can remember going into my father's work with him one evening. You could just see how well he treated others and how they trusted him. You can learn so much from observing parents. I would see him at family gatherings, and he was always connecting, and finding common ground, with others.'

Gareth's positive experience of seeing trust close up was reaffirmed, rather than damaged, when he entered professional football. When he joined Aston Villa, the captain of the team Andy Townsend proactively sought him out, welcomed him and helped him settle into the new club. Similarly, when Gareth made the England national team one of the senior players, Stuart Pearce, took him under his wing in that potentially intimidating environment.

Those experiences have moulded the relational philosophy that Gareth describes in this way:

'I think it's crucial to have an understanding of what the world is like for the people who are working with you. I want to understand what makes people different, to appreciate diversity in their backgrounds and upbringing. I think in the old days in football, everybody thought you've got to treat people the same, because that's fair. But to get the best out of people you have to treat them all differently because we are all individuals.'[108]

6.3 back to belonging

In Chapter 2, we visited an England rugby team dinner in October 2013 where Stuart Lancaster and I presented to the team a version of its Us story.

Another ancestor the team met that evening was Jimmy Peters.

Jimmy was the first black player to represent the England rugby team. He did that in 1906 – seventy-two years before Viv Anderson became the first black player selected in the England men's football team.

Jimmy was born in Manchester in 1879 to a West Indian father and English mother. He spent much of his childhood in a travelling circus with his family. His father was a lion tamer and his brother an acrobat. When Jimmy was old enough, he became a bare-back horse rider.

Tragically, Jimmy's father was one day mauled to death by a lion. Jimmy stayed on with the circus until age eleven, when he was abandoned by it after breaking his arm. He was taken in by a local resident of the town the circus had been performing in, who then arranged for him to be sent to an orphanage in Greenwich, London.

Jimmy was introduced to rugby by being allowed, as an orphan, free admission to watch the famous Blackheath club play in south London. Soon, he played the game himself at school.

At nineteen, Jimmy left London for Bristol and played for the prestigious city club. In the seasons that followed he was selected to play for the Devon county side and then on 17 March 1906 Jimmy played his first international for England against Scotland in Edinburgh. England won in a surprise result. A week later Jimmy was a star in the team's 35–8 win over France in Paris.

Later that same year, on 17 October 1906, Jimmy lined up for the Devon county side to play the visiting South African Springboks in front of twenty thousand people at Devonport. Devon were the champion county of England and Jimmy the star player.

Before the match started, Springboks captain Paul Roos advised the referee that his team would not play against a black player. The Devon captain stood his ground and said that if Jimmy couldn't play, then the rest of the team wouldn't either. The issue was only defused when the South African High Commissioner to the United Kingdom came down from the stand and persuaded Roos to concede the point. The Springboks played the match under protest.

Jimmy went on to play four more internationals for England over the next two seasons. Then, he suffered a serious injury at work, losing three fingers. That spelled the end of his international career. Jimmy managed to return to club rugby a few years later and played professional rugby league for a short time.

Jimmy spent the rest of his working life as a carpenter in the Bristol dockyards. He died in 1954 aged seventy-four.

I told Jimmy's story with an evocative colourised photo of him wearing his England shirt as the backdrop.

As the story was told, I noticed how a number of players in the team physically leaned in as they met their ancestor Jimmy Peters.

Five days later, the *Daily Telegraph* wrote an article about a new player to the England team, Billy Vunipola. Billy was born in Australia to Tongan parents and moved to the United Kingdom as a young child, schooled first in Wales and then in England. In the interview Billy talked about the dinner that week and said:

'It [Jimmy's story] struck a chord because it was about how accepted people felt coming to England, and that is how me and my brother have felt. That is why the story touched me. I definitely feel part of that English tradition.'[109]

Jimmy's story took less than ten minutes to tell. It resonated a lot longer.

It was a piece of intentional leadership by Stuart Lancaster that accelerated the transition of Billy and other players from feeling like outsiders to belonging. Through storytelling, natural fear and anxiety were reduced and the seeds of deep trust sown.

6.4 face time

*You never really understand a person until you consider
things from his point of view . . . Until you climb inside
of his skin and walk around in it.*
Atticus Finch in *To Kill a Mockingbird* by Harper Lee

American leadership coach and author Marshall Goldsmith has
a saying: *Leadership is a contact sport.* So much truth in that.

Time together goes a long way to building trust. Not just in
words exchanged but the experience of being physically together.
In well-designed shared experiences, stress reduces while endorphins and oxytocin are released. This strengthens the social
bonds in teams.

There is an important gender difference here. Studies by
Oxford University show that conversation is a significant enabler
of social bonding in females but less so in males. Instead, males'
social bonding and trust building is significantly enhanced by
'doing stuff' together.[110]

I recall a camp with a team before a World Cup which reaffirmed this male trait. The team enjoyed each other's company,
less so long meetings. Our camp was themed *We have everything
we need.* In the morning we split into small groups and went
into the countryside to locate food we would cook together that

evening: some guys hunted deer, others fished on a lake, some went crayfishing on the sea; a few went picking vegetables and wild berries and some went into village butchers and bakeries. Late in the afternoon we all came back together and the food we'd sourced was laid out. Another group of guys then went into the hotel kitchen and worked with the chefs on preparing the meal. That evening, everyone enjoyed a wonderful dinner together. The only words spoken as a group were a few toasts. After dinner, the team settled in for an hour of singing. It was a day where endorphins, oxytocin and dopamine spiked with few words spoken.

I am not sure how well understood and factored into building trust these gender differences are, particularly in mixed-gender teams.

International footballer Ali Riley shared with me:

'I've had experiences where a male coach has come in and told us that we needed to focus on the tactical and technical and should reduce the time we spent in meetings connecting with each other. But for us, it was really important before games to speak together about our purpose and what we stood for as a team, our values. This is what really made us strong. It was our X factor.'

A constant truth, though, is that for both genders, quality conversations go a long way to building trust between individuals. They provide signals of authenticity, tribal loyalty and empathy. They also enable us to better interpret and understand others' personality quirks. This then helps fine-tune our ability to predict one another.

Another way in which these conversations are beneficial is in helping to diffuse what is known as the 'fundamental attribution error'. This is the tendency we have to attribute what we perceive as poor behaviours of others to their personality, while blaming our own poor behaviours on the context and environment we found ourselves in. This is a potentially corrosive factor in team dynamics as it drives distrust. Empathy and understanding make it more likely that we will process 'below the line' behaviours of others in a way that does not damage trust.

There is, therefore, no substitute for face time, no matter how busy you are, and there are few busier than the generals who run NATO's military operations.

I was fortunate enough to work with the sixteenth Command Group of NATO when they carved out time from their punishing schedules, which includes monthly personal briefings at the White House, to strengthen their connection and trust.

The three four-star generals that comprise NATO's Command Group are responsible for the alliance's military operations. Each general has their own extensive staff and significant workload. Whilst the generals would meet periodically, joined by their staff, time had not been specifically carved out to deepen their personal relationships. This is what I was invited to facilitate.

I believe simplicity tends to be the best approach so when we met up at a secured venue, I asked each general in turn to simply share their personal story on how they got to be around this table.

Admiral Jim Stavridis, the Supreme Allied Commander of Europe, went first.

He told a version of his own *whakapapa*. He started with the story of his paternal grandparents. How his grandfather,

Dimitrios Stavridis, was an ethnic Greek schoolteacher in Anatolia in Turkey. How in the early 1920s, with the breakdown of the Ottoman Empire and ethnic cleansing rampant, his grandfather fled his home in Turkey and, in a small boat from the port of Smyrna, made his way across the Aegean Sea to Athens.

Jim Stavridis explained how his grandfather's brother was killed by the Turks in the violence that ensued. In Athens, the daily sailing schedule of the port dictated his grandfather's destination for his new life. The ship he could first book a ticket on was leaving for New York. Upon arrival, like millions of others, he was processed on Ellis Island and became a citizen of the United States.

Jim Stavridis then spoke of how his father had joined the Marine Corps and served in the Second World War, Korea and Vietnam.

He took his time as he explained how when he first became a naval commander, he was assigned a billion-dollar destroyer and ordered to take part in an exercise in the Mediterranean.

He spoke with emotion as he described his first orders as commander being delivered to his house and his opening the envelope. The port his destroyer would be based at was Izmir, previously named Smyrna – the very same place his grandfather had fled for his life in a refugee raft seventy years before.

Sir Richard Shirreff, the four-star British General and Deputy Supreme Allied Commander for Europe, then shared his own remarkable story. He began with a revelation: 'I am actually an African.'

Sir Richard explained how he had grown up in Kenya, living in a series of remote parts of the country while his father served as an administrator. He spoke about how much he'd loved the people of the country and the outdoor adventurous life he had enjoyed growing up. He talked about how hard he had found it when the family relocated to live in England; that he did not feel that he 'fitted in'.

Sir Richard described going back to Kenya many years later and being hit with a powerful sense of belonging.

When he talked through his personal journey (public school, Oxford University, Sandhurst) he spoke with great humility in that although these were all prestigious institutions, this nagging feeling of being an outsider had followed him around. He said it was not until he joined the King's Royal Hussars, eventually becoming its Commanding Officer, that he felt another genuine sense of belonging in his life. He spoke about how that regiment was family and those connections lifelong. It was deeply emotional listening to this. Sir Richard then rounded out his story describing his other high-profile commands in the British Army (humbly leaving out being knighted in 2010).

German Air Force four-star General Manfred Lange then spoke powerfully about his early life in post-war West Germany and how that had fuelled a motivation to follow a career that would help him to ensure that the horrific legacy of suffering he had witnessed growing up would not be repeated.

The three men then, for the first time, went to a private room and lunched together without any staff present. I left them alone for this and overheard a lot of laughter as they ate together.

Sir Richard looks back on that session:

'Reflecting years later, your session enabled us to see each other as we really were: not four-star military commanders with the trappings and badges of high rank but men whose early years growing up had shaped them irrevocably. Opening up to each other in that way highlighted our respective vulnerabilities and helped us to better understand each other – and ourselves. Without understanding and empathy there cannot be trust.'

What later occurred to me was how much the way in which the generals had told their stories mirrored Māori custom.

Pepeha is a traditional way of introducing yourself. It starts with your connection to the land and then works through your tribe and kin affiliations ending with yourself. Without any prompting from me, this is how each of the generals went about sharing their own stories: their spiritual 'land', boats that crossed oceans, their kin and military tribe, their careers to this point.

It once again reaffirmed how much traditional wisdom is universal in nature.

Such sharing is particularly beneficial the more diverse a team is. Within one team conversation, I have heard someone describe their privileged background (private schooling, elite coaching, great mentoring) followed by a teammate who described growing up in a poverty-ravaged ghetto where gangs bet on children's street games and threatened families where the children didn't follow instructions to cheat. Through carving out time to connect in this way, these teams give themselves an opportunity to understand and trust each other on a much deeper level.

A person can, of course, never fully reveal themselves in such conversations and sessions. However, they just need to give enough of themselves for others to hold on to.

6.5 freedom to play

When my daughter, Livvy, was six years old she started weekend ballet classes. Livvy's a naturally social and enthusiastic soul. She loves moving, she loves activities, she loves being around her friends, she loves being taught. However, she didn't enjoy ballet classes. Each week they were invariably preceded by angst and followed by a sense of relief.

It was hard to work out why there was so much anxiety around these classes. Nothing terrible ever seemed to happen, and Livvy would say that the teachers and the other children were nice. Yet her anxiety persisted. The only clue was in the way she described the classes as 'strict and scary'. I connected this to a cascade of conformity from her compulsory pink tutu, to her hair having to be tied up in a bun, to the precise technical positions, to the regimented format of the classes.

Coincidentally, that same year I was invited to work in an elite ballet environment. My brief was to immerse myself in their performance culture and share my observations as an outsider.

After that project, I got to know and spend time with some world-class ballet performers, looking at the world of ballet through their eyes.

I came to form a view on what triggered Livvy's anxiety. She felt that her freedom to play and be herself was crushed by an unrelenting demand to conform. Her spirit was being repressed.

Our ancestors have taught us that humans flourish when we are in spiritual balance: the *yin* and *yang* – light and dark – energy that comes from opposing forces that become complementary when in balance.

In teams, this manifests itself in a harmony between boundaries and autonomy. Boundaries keep us safe and provide clarity, which lowers anxiety and enhances trust. Autonomy unlocks intrinsic motivation by giving us a sense of control and self-determination. Being given a sense of autonomy also signals that our leaders trust us, which, again, reduces our anxiety levels.

As Daniel Pink puts it in *Drive*:

Human beings have an innate inner drive to be autonomous, self-determined, and connected to one another . . . The opposite of autonomy is control. And since they sit at different poles of the behavioural compass, they point us toward different destinations. Control leads to compliance; autonomy leads to engagement.[111]

For Livvy, no sense of autonomy, or freedom to play, was present. What she was experiencing was just anxiety around conforming the whole time and avoiding correction (shaming) in front of her friends. That wasn't making for a joyful experience.

Our ancestors passed down with care the need for balance between boundaries and autonomy. In my own culture, two ancestral ideas that hold deep resonance with me are *tapu* and *noa*. *Tapu* describes those aspects of life that are sacred, restricted, prescribed and non-negotiable (this includes protocols around entering a meeting house and dealing with a death). *Noa*, in contrast, describes those parts of life where there are no such 'rules' and we are free to determine how we express ourselves.

Tapu and *noa* drive trust by providing clarity of what is expected in the environment. When everyone understands and complies with what is *tapu* then we can more confidently predict the behaviour of others. Similarly, when we know what areas of life are *noa* then we can respect others' self-expression.

When there is too much *tapu*, then trust is compromised by the individual's anxiety of not having a sense of autonomy. It sends signals they are not trusted.

When there is too much *noa*, then the environment can become chaotic, confusing and impossible to predict what others will do, as they're making it up as they go.

It is the balance between boundaries and autonomy, between *tapu* and *noa*, that produces nurturing conditions for trust to exist.

I use these concepts in all of my work. In every team or organisation, we identify what is *tapu* – what is sacred and non-negotiable in this team – and what is *noa* – the spaces where individuals are free to express themselves. This harmony is for me critical in establishing an environment where people can thrive.

In ballet culture, my impression is that there is a lot of *tapu* and not so much *noa* – environments are skewed towards strict boundaries and conformity. This in turn generates high levels of anxiety and hurts the building of trust.

One of this generation's best-known male ballet dancers, Sergei Polunin, said exactly that when he walked out of his role as principal at the Royal Ballet Company aged only twenty-two. The reasons he gave read as code for this imbalance:

'I never had any freedom – over my whole life, there had always been people telling me what to do. And when I did finally get that freedom. I had no idea what to do with it – that was something I hadn't been trained for.'[112]

Polunin later stated he felt 'like a prisoner'.[113]

Another world-class ballet dancer I have got to know is current male principal at the Royal Ballet Company Steven McRae.

Steven has experienced many incredible highs and lows in his career and is uniquely positioned to reflect on this tension that sits at the heart of ballet.

Steven, an Australian, grew up in a working-class family in the western suburbs of Sydney. His father worked as an auto electrician and the family's weekends were typically spent at a motor racing track. Steven discovered dance when he was seven.

Given his modest background, Steven understood from an early age that if he was to make a career in ballet, he would need to forge his way by excelling in exams and winning competitions in Sydney and then nationwide. This became his childhood.

The complexity and stress of this life really registered for Steven when he was ten years old. He entered a national ballet competition, where the winner would travel overseas to learn and compete. Steven was announced as runner-up. After the announcement, some of the judges came over to Steven's parents and explained to them that he had actually been awarded most points and it had been decided that he was the winner. However, the organisers had unilaterally changed the result based on 'other considerations'. That is a lot for a kid to take. As Steven puts it now:

'At a very young age I was blatantly exposed to the idea that it is not always about who is best on the day. Trust was blown out by that experience.'

When Steven was sixteen years old, he set his heart on studying at the famous Royal Ballet School in London:

'Financially, there was no way we could ever afford that. I knew I would have to win some of these competitions.'

An international Royal Academy of Dancing competition was held at the Sydney Opera House that year. This was an opportunity for Steven to gain a profile beyond Australia and open up opportunities abroad.

'I felt immense pressure – being compared to others from around the world every second of that week; needing this to open doors.'

Steven won the gold medal.

That success funded Steven, then seventeen, to travel to Switzerland to compete at the prestigious *Prix de Lausanne*. This competition not only had a trophy and prize money but scholarships to prestigious ballet schools and apprenticeships to professional companies. Steven travelled to Switzerland with his mother. Neither had been to Europe before. In the course of that week, Steven's mother began to suffer from a stress-related illness and was hospitalised:

'I was terrified, absolutely terrified, but I learned that I was good at hiding it. I had to step on that stage looking indestructible. My mentality was that I was either going to sink or swim.'

Steven won first place at the *Prix de Lausanne* and got to fulfil his dream of attending the Royal Ballet School. He and his mother flew directly to London from Lausanne. Not being able to afford to stay in a hotel to settle Steven in, his mother flew back to Australia after a few days.

Steven's place at the school was not open for six months. Without knowing anyone in London, he boarded in a hostel in Hampstead, sharing a room.

During Steven's eighteen months at the Royal Ballet School there was constant pressure to impress teachers, casting in school performances and then applying for jobs with world-leading companies. For over two years he was beset with homesickness. In his final term, a position was confirmed for Steven at the Royal Ballet Company.

Within five years, at age twenty-three, Steven was appointed male principal dancer at the Royal Ballet.

The demands of the elite ballet life are relentless. There is a constant need to prove yourself, no matter who you are, and retain favour with directors and choreographers.

There is constant internal competition for roles and recognition between the dancers themselves. I have heard many times the haunting term 'frenemy'.

There is also the constant spectre of significant injury, time away rehabilitating and having to re-establish yourself upon your return.

Steven has three times experienced and overcome potential career-ending injuries. In October 2019 upon returning from a series of leg injuries and operations, he ruptured his achilles tendon while performing on stage at the Royal Opera House in *Manon*.

Despite being titled, at thirty-four, *the hottest man in ballet* by *The Times*, Steven has had to start over again and re-establish his career.

Steven explains this never-ending anxiety:

'Everyone is climbing for the top rank, but once you get there you're surrounded by others at a similar level. Even there you still feel constantly vulnerable – who is flavour of the month? Does the director like me or them? Who does the company want to push in the public eye? What does this choreographer prefer? Will I lose my place on the ladder after injury?'

As a highly prescribed art form, language pervades ballet around pursuing 'perfection'. As Steven puts it:

'We look at ourselves in the mirror twenty-four hours a day constantly striving for this impossible perfection.'

This inherent anxiety is in stark contrast to the pleadings of modern researchers such as Brené Brown:

'And we perfect, most dangerously, our children. Let me tell you what we think about children. They're hardwired for struggle when they get here. And when you hold those perfect little babies in your hand, our job is not to say, "Look at her, she's perfect. My job is just to keep her perfect." That's not our job. Our job is to look and say, "You know what? You're imperfect, and you're wired for struggle, but you are worthy of love and belonging." That's our job.'[114]

This is not the traditional style of teaching and directing in ballet. Instead, it is highly directive, often blunt and with a perceived love more for the art than the dancer. In Eric Blondeau's terms, *emotional availability* is often missing.

So much *tapu*, so little *noa*. Steven describes it in this way:

'I call it the teacher-student mentality. As a professional you're still treated as a student – "Today you will do this, today you will rehearse this, you will do a full run even though there is a performance tomorrow." There's little consideration of the athlete and dancer. Now as an experienced principal I have the ability to challenge what's being demanded. However, most ballet dancers won't have the confidence to do that.'

This formality carries over into how feedback is given, or, as it is known, 'corrections'. Traditionally, this is matter of fact and detached, rather than guided learning. Former principal at both the Royal Danish Ballet and the Royal Ballet Company, Nehemiah Kish, put it to me in this way:

'You're always being judged and evaluated. You need as a professional to get past that and not continually seek approval.'

251

This absence of explicit signals of caring compromises trust being established.

As a result, performers develop a mindset of not showing vulnerability. They predict that any perceived physical or emotional 'weakness' could be held against them – a cultural thread exists that part of 'making it' is the ability to suffer in silence and hide emotion. Steven explains:

'There is a mentality of not showing weakness. For many years you received medical treatment for an injury and you freaked out that management would find out. The culture of ballet celebrates those who can function like a machine.'

A comment that unnerved me when I spoke with ballet performers was how many potentially great dancers they mentioned had fallen by the wayside. Some modest enough to suggest that better dancers than themselves simply couldn't cope with the demands. That the ballet way was 'survival of the fittest'.

Environments that are spiritually out of balance are breeding grounds for intimidation, bullying and misused power. This lies beneath scandals, such as allegations of physical and emotional abuse in elite-level gymnastics.

Often the narrative presented is of a rogue individual who has been identified and removed. To properly address the real issues requires confronting the ecosystem in which such toxic behaviours appeared.

It is not the presence of stress and competition that is the issue – it is how the environment frames the experience and the sense of wellbeing and trust that generates.

Ballet brings incredible joy, satisfaction and camaraderie to thousands. It also carries higher levels of anxiety and lower levels of trust than many feel is safe. As Steven concludes:

'It is up to my generation to bring in change. It is an incredible profession and wonderful privilege. But the culture of ballet can be reset.'

As the generation of Steven, Nehemiah Kish and Yuhui Choe soon step up to lead, they can be guided by ancestral ideas such as *tapu* and *noa*. They will find a better balance between boundaries and autonomy without compromising the quality of classical ballet.

That future is in plain sight. Yuhui Choe identifies this irony:

'Although there is constant pressure to conform, the most celebrated dancers are the ones unafraid to break the rules and be themselves. They are the ones who emotionally connect with the audience.'

The public see their spirit freed.

6.6 the dividend

Stress exists in all relationships. As no two minds are the same there will always be degrees of misalignment and differences of opinion. In teams, social anxiety adds a whole new level. Not only are we seeking to get on with others, but we are constantly socially anxious around our sense of belonging and our status.

As Eric Blondeau puts it, 'The only real psychological safety is when you are dead.'

This underlying emotional edge complicates speaking honestly in teams, giving and taking feedback and addressing issues that are holding back the collective mission.

Trust is the key differentiator between teams who walk towards challenging conversations and those who avoid them.

Trust allows individuals to speak without fear of reprisals. They can confidently predict that participating in challenging conversations is safe in this environment.

In order to get to this point, teams have to overcome our inbuilt bias to conformity. We have a biological stress response when at odds with our group – a primal fear of shaming, punishment or even rejection.

Studies show that it takes less than two hundred milliseconds to register that the group has come up with a different answer than our own – then less than half a second for us to conform to their position.[115]

As Robert Sapolsky puts it:

Like so many other animals, we have an often frantic need to conform, belong and obey . . . When we discover we are out of step with everyone else, our amygdalae spasm with anxiety, our memories are revised, and our sensory processing regions are even pressured to experience what is not true. All to fit in.[116]

Laid on top of these evolved biological responses, many cultural practices undermine a fully honest environment.

I grew up in a culture where displaying emotion was crazily associated with weakness and discouraged. Instead, emotions were 'bottled up', leading to either silence or an overreaction later.

Many cultures instil a deep belief that you respect your elders and those of higher status. This translates into deference. Therefore, the idea of speaking openly feels counter to that belief system.

Teams can also have an unwritten 'good guy / gal' culture where there is a premium on being 'positive' and 'inoffensive'. That is another element that can get in the way of difficult conversations.

Our ancestors understood the fears and anxiety caused by the prospect of challenging others. In *Hagakure*, the book of the Samurai, written around 1716 by Yamamoto Tsunetomo, there is a section dedicated to how to challenge others in the right way (without shaming them). Our Japanese ancestors emphasised trust as the starting point for safe challenge: *Strive to become a trusted colleague and ensure that he has faith in your words.*[117]

If a team truly aspires to be high performing, they have to find a way to get good at feedback, challenge sub-standard behaviours and address issues that are 'slowing the boat down'. I agree with University of Texas basketball coach Shaka Smart:

'The most important component of accelerating growth is changing someone's relationship with feedback.'[118]

This involves being able to treat feedback as data. That requires trust and maturity.

Safe challenge is enhanced when it becomes part of the team's identity: *this is who we are, this is how we do things, we expect this of each other.* This part of our Us story wrapped in accounts of where it existed and helped us and where it was neglected and hurt us.

In Chapter 3, we tracked the journey of the South African cricket team's Protea Fire Culture. This work included extracting what they value (their values) from their Us story. One of those values was *honesty.*

The need for the Proteas to address this issue was obvious in an early encounter with the team when one of the coaches privately came to me and described his relationship with one of the team's star players. He explained how he perceived the player was not fully fit and was withholding this from him and team management. He described to me his inability to communicate openly and honestly with this player. His anxiety was that if he challenged the player, then it could damage their relationship (and with it his own job security). This fear of a difficult conversation outweighed the potential team benefit in addressing an important issue.

He asked if I would speak with the player to establish what was going on with him and whether he had some undisclosed issues. I respectfully declined the invitation. Instead, we put a circle around this issue as a priority for the team leadership to address.

The issue within the team was not that dishonesty prevailed. It was a fear of conversations that would have an emotional edge. The net result was that important conversations necessary to help the team weren't happening.

The tortured history of South Africa added complexity. Each person in the team was connected to a side during the apartheid era – the oppressors and the oppressed. Therefore, in the early days at least, there was a deeper symbolism beneath challenging each other that simply doesn't exist in most teams.

We created a space at Hennops River to address this as a team.

I led with a reflection of how they represent a nation that many believed averted a civil war in its transformation to democracy, at least in part due to the Truth and Reconciliation Commission chaired by Archbishop Desmond Tutu.

We discussed how the Truth and Reconciliation Commission invited victims of human rights violations to give evidence about their experiences. The Commission held over one thousand hearings listening to citizens and permanently recording their evidence.

The Truth and Reconciliation Commission was a uniquely

South African creation. It put honesty above all else in a spirit of forgiveness and reconciliation (rather than fear of punishment).

It begged the rhetorical question for the Proteas: *As a team that represents this nation, why would we have a lower standard*?

Honesty, and everything that entailed, became a deeply held team value, emerging from, and part of, the team's wider Us story.

From this strong foundation, the team embarked on a journey of learning how to truly embrace safe challenge and conflict in a demanding, fast-paced, high-pressure environment.

The fourth captain to lead the Protea Fire Culture was Faf du Plessis.

Faf was appointed to lead the team in 2016. His first task was to reconnect them to the Protea Fire Culture and get them back on track.

A major focus for Faf in this period of renewal was taking the value of honesty to another level:

'Honesty had deep personal meaning for me. I was a born-again Christian and part of that process was an audit on where I was as a person. That had exposed some gaps around my own honesty at times. As captain of the team it was important that I lived this value.'

Within the team at that time there were various places where safe challenge had slipped. Some players, who had been good friends, had fallen out many months before and that tension was heavy in the dressing room. Some lowering of team standards had crept in when the losses came. There was a gap between the 'team first' talk some players spoke in public and more self-interested behaviours behind the scenes. None of these issues had been addressed as the team slid in its performances and world ranking.

In the Fairway camp we sat as a team to work through this. Places of pain within the team came to the surface. In the safe place that was made, differences of opinion were aired and common ground found. Away from that space, I took the team management and player leaders away. I had them go around the table giving each other feedback on the past twelve months. In smaller circles, over a few days, staff and players invited individuals to meet with them and work through tensions.

Although the team culture had drifted, as honesty was a team value that had been celebrated in the past, it was not difficult to resurrect the desired behaviours and get back on track.

Within six months the team would rise from seventh to regain their number one world ranking.

As the team's leader, Faf led by his actions.

If there was an issue that needed addressing, Faf would raise it but always with compassion and care. Most times, that would involve a private conversation, other times it would be raised in the team space but without shaming anyone.

One evening in Colombo, Sri Lanka, I asked some guys across the diversity of the team to share with the others what the world looked like through their eyes. Life experiences and spiritual beliefs were shared. As well as deepening understanding and empathy, their vulnerability sent a strong signal that it was okay to speak honestly and allow emotion to sit between them.

Then Faf, with considerable vulnerability of his own, shared why honesty had such deep personal meaning for him, identifying painful examples from his life. He gave everyone in the team an open invitation to speak honestly with him about anything.

At the start of each new season, and each major series, the Proteas would take time out to reconnect to the Protea Fire Culture and the value of honesty was always checked and reset.

The aspiration was to create a competitive advantage through their ability to give and take feedback and discuss issues as a team.

What we quickly learned was that this value of honesty required training to hone it as a skill and habit. Space was made to drive awareness about the natural emotion and discomfort around confronting others. From there, a safe way for the team to speak up and challenge each other was found. This initially involved a scenario whereby someone wishing to challenge another would go about it in this sort of way: *Hey, can we chat? Today out there I think I saw X which looked below the line we've set. I could be completely wrong so just tell me if I am. Just trying to grow together, brother.* It was important to have some form of template in these early stages until habits became ingrained and individuals developed their own styles.

Crucially, Faf realised that to truly drive safe challenge, the most critical element was that team members felt they could do this peer to peer. It was a lived value when the players themselves would role-model and police it, without the need for an authority figure. That insight reflects important work from psychologist Judith Rich Harris showing that from early years the people who have the most influence on our behaviour are probably our peers, not our parents or other authority figures.

Faf reflects back now on the team's journey of finding a way to safely challenge each other and the status quo:

'I learned that there is no perfection when it comes to an honest environment. You cannot be extreme and share every feeling and thought. It needs to be targeted around things that need to be said to make the boat go faster. Room has to be made for the fact that different personalities have different appetites for giving and taking challenge. What was important was that we lived it together.'

Over time, the players themselves came to associate this value of speaking openly and honestly with belonging to this team.

unleashed

Players don't remember what you say in team talks or practices – what they do remember is how you made them feel.

Sir Alf Ramsey (manager of 1966
England World Cup winning football team)

7.1 the difference

When my father died, I attended a small rural school, a few miles from the southern coast of the island. I turned six the week after he passed. My schoolteacher that year was Jim Watson. He was twenty-five and recently married to his high school sweetheart Julianne. Later that same year, two other children in my class also lost their fathers, both commercial fishermen drowned in a severe storm. That was a lot of pain for a small community. It was also a lot of pain for their young teacher.

The following year we moved up to the next class. Jim Watson kept looking out for me and the others. He sensed there could be benefit in me spending time in a different environment. He asked my mother whether it would be all right if I stayed the occasional weekend with him and Julianne. My mother agreed and this became part of the rhythm of our lives through the next decade. The Watsons invited me to join them on holidays as well – this young couple, without children at the time, having me tag along.

With them I got to spend time in the mountains and lakes of the hinterland. Sometimes staying in a family holiday house, other times caravans and hunting huts. Experiences I would not otherwise have had.

The Watsons provided a space freed from grief, where a sense of optimism could breathe. Conversations were based on possibilities rather than constraints. Patiently they would lead me into considering the years ahead and we would rehearse the options and decisions that awaited. This became a vision of the future that I followed.

It was an early, and incredibly fortunate, lesson in how transformative an environment can be.

Over forty years later, each time I return to my hometown, visiting Jim and Julianne comes straight after seeing my family. Even now, after a short catch-up, the conversation quickly moves on to *what comes next*.

7.2 transformed

Andrew 'Son' White came to understand the transformative power of environment too.

We were born a few miles apart. We attended the same high school. We played for the same rugby club. We grew up on and around farms. What most distanced us was time. Son died three weeks after I was born.

When Son was twelve, in 1906, he passed national exams with merit to secure his place at Southland Boys' High School. This was a significant moment for Son's working-class family as entry to this school opened up a potential route to university study and a profession, not a path previously traversed by his family.

However, the following year, his first at high school, tragedy struck when Son's father died. He had been self-employed, and in those days before social welfare, his early death put the family in economic peril. Son was informed by his mother that after just two terms of high school he would need to leave and find work. At thirteen, Son left school and became a farm labourer, living away from home.

This was Son's life for the next seven years. Hard work, a stolen education and the chance to just be a kid denied him by circumstance. His one day a week off work was spent fishing or tending to the renowned horses bred on the farm.

On 4 August 1914 Great Britain declared war on Germany,

marking the commencement of the First World War. New Zealand automatically followed. The following week, Son, twenty years old now, enlisted.

Son was gifted a horse by the farmer he worked for and joined up with the region's mounted rifles regiment. He took his horse with him to military training and then on the ship the regiment took to Egypt and eventually to the Western Front in France. In December 1914 Son and his regiment disembarked in Alexandria in Egypt and travelled by train to their training base on the outskirts of Cairo.

On 20 May 1915 Son and his comrades set off for the beaches of Gallipoli. There they joined the surviving forces that had first arrived on 25 April – marked sacred in our country as Anzac Day. Out in the waters off the peninsula was a Royal Navy ship, *HMS Blenheim*, which my English grandfather would soon join.

Of the eight hundred men in Son's regiment who landed at Gallipoli only five officers and ten soldiers were still fit to fight by the time they were evacuated off the peninsula that December.

The worst moment for the regiment came on 28 August 1915 when they were ordered to attack Hill 60. Sixty-five of Son's mates were killed in fifteen minutes as they charged Turkish machine guns with fixed bayonets. Son himself was hospitalised for three months on a nearby island during the Gallipoli ordeal. This attack was part of General Sir Ian Hamilton's failed 'August Offensive' and was ordered by General Sir William Birdwood.[119] The surviving men never forgave those British generals for ordering this suicidal assault.

Because of the destruction of Son's regiment, the surviving

men were redeployed to other army units. Son joined the field artillery and was directly sent to the Western Front. Over the following three years Son would fight in the battles of the Somme, Messines and Passchendaele.

As a skilled horseman, Son was designated a driver and was responsible for managing the horses that moved the guns to new deployments and supplied ammunition. This involved hooking twenty horses on to each gun and leading them forward through the mud and torn roads.

The work was gruelling given the incessant shelling they were exposed to and horrendous unnavigable conditions. An officer in Son's regiment recorded in the official divisional journal:

> The men suffered from constant exposure to the heavy rain, were up to their knees in mud, and slept in it when they got time to sleep. Under the weeping skies in the battlefield, with its battered trenches and tangle of broken wire, its debris of smashed transport, dead horses and unburied men presented a scene of desolation, suffering and death that must have awakened sombre and questioning thought in the mind of even the most war-hardened soldier as to the end and the purpose and the meaning of it all.[120]

In June 1918 a medical board, at Étaples in France, declared Son unfit for further service as he was suffering from 'shell shock'. Shell shock is a post-traumatic stress disorder that occurs in combat conditions and causes mental injury. Son's symptoms included uncontrollable shaking, a resting pulse rate of ninety-two, impaired hearing and shortness of breath. Son returned home by ship, arriving exactly one month before Armistice Day.

The army's medical board decided that Son, twenty-four now, could be cared for by his family instead of being sent to a psychiatric hospital. Upon returning to our hometown, Son was examined by another medical board who deemed him 'greatly affirmed'. He was officially designated as disabled and provided with a state pension. He was tended to at home by his mother and sisters.

The following year, 1919, the White family was contacted by the Carswells. A generation before, Son's father had been business partners with Hugh Carswell. Three of Hugh's sons now ran the family stock and station business Carswell & Co. A fourth son, James, had been killed in the Battle of Passchendaele, which Son had also fought in.

The Carswell brothers had heard of Son's circumstances and wanted to help him. They invited Son to get out of the family home and come to their warehouse to do odd jobs, such as sweeping up at the end of the day.

This environment and this experience would be transformative for Son.

The Carswell brothers were known as gregarious and humorous characters and the workplace reflected their personality. The sense of belonging to this vibrant place had an immediate impact on Son.

His severe symptoms miraculously reduced within months. Alongside an unanticipated physical recovery, Son regained a sense of value and dignity.

Some of his new work colleagues played rugby for a local club and invited Son to attend training: as a way of getting fit, socialising with them and meeting new people. Son, now twenty-five, had never played organised sport before. During the war, he had watched rugby played by soldiers from the sidelines but never taken part.

Son attended the club's training nights. Soon, this became another place he felt he fitted in, that he belonged. Some other players were also returning soldiers. Work and now the club were places where Son could be with others who understood and accepted the darkness of his experiences.

As it happened, Son was a natural player. He was quickly selected for the club's first team. By the end of that initial season he had made the provincial team. Within two years, Son was selected for the national team, the All Blacks, to play South Africa in their first ever international match on 13 August 1921.

All of this occurred in less than three years of Son's return home with shell shock and being officially classified as disabled.

How different Son's life would have been if, firstly, he'd been sent to a psychiatric hospital instead of his family home. Then, if the Carswell brothers had not been driven by empathy to offer him part-time work.

In these environments, Son was able to shed labels put on him by doctors and bureaucratic boards, and transform himself through a sense of belonging and optimism.

Son White would go on to play for the All Blacks for another four years and become a key player in the undefeated 1924 Invincibles team's tour to the United Kingdom and France.

In a remarkable twist of fate, on that 1924 All Blacks tour, the British Olympic Association hosted a dinner for the team at the Piccadilly Hotel. The guests of honour at the dinner included Sir Ian Hamilton and Sir William Birdwood, the same British generals responsible for the attack against the Turks at Gallipoli that had decimated Son's regiment. He was personally introduced to them; he shook their hands, looked them in the eye and then moved on.

Later on the same tour, in Paris early in 1925, Son would similarly be introduced to the architect of the Gallipoli campaign, Winston Churchill, during a formal function.

That same week the All Blacks visited First World War gravesites, laying wreaths at the grave of 1905 Originals All Blacks captain Dave Gallaher. The team visited the sites of battles that Son, and some other teammates, had fought a mere eight years before.

Son's life could have been so completely different.

Michael Gervais defines optimism as a mindset of 'something good is about to happen'.

Where we sit between optimism and pessimism is heavily shaped by our environments and our tribes. It is this which embeds itself in our own sense of identity – the future in which we see ourselves.

When I look down my lines of people, my *whakapapa*, I see a back and forth of achievement and suffering but most of all I see an unbroken line into the future. As I trace the moving sun, I take great comfort in knowing that when the sun arrived on each generation, our ancestors built an optimistic vision of what we could be.

Something good is waiting ahead of us . . .

7.3 contagion

No man is an island,
entire of itself

John Donne, 'Meditation 17' (1623)

CAUSE AND EFFECT

The ancient Polynesian navigators were more interested in cause and effect than objective measurement. They may not have known how many miles lay between two islands, but they understood the impact of winds, currents and tides on the direction they were pursuing.

Over recent centuries we have developed a strong bias towards valuing what we can measure and devaluing what we can't. The scientific method has encouraged us to see the world as mechanical systems that can be reduced to constituent parts. The Industrial Revolution replicated this in how *homo sapiens* worked together – the production line mentality.

What may have been lost is clarity on causal relationships. Cause and effect that our ancestors saw clearly, we have perhaps lost sight of.

We are not machines. We do not perform tasks in a vacuum. We are profoundly affected by the environment we are in and particularly by those around us. Teamwork is a dynamic and complex system, not a linear process.

We know this in our daily lives. The mood or mindset of one family member can dramatically change the group dynamic and influence the behaviour of every other individual. I've long been aware of my own acute sensitivity to environment – how often my own 'performance' seemed less about my abilities and more about the environment I found myself in.

I have heard one of Britain's leading sports psychologists declare that 70 per cent of human behaviour is influenced by our environment. This insight reflects work in the 1930s by psychologist Kurt Lewin in his equation: $b=f(p,e)$ where *behaviour* (b) is a function of the interaction between the *person* (p) and their *environment* (e).

Writer on organisational management Ralph Stacey puts it this way:

The . . . mind is not an 'it' located and stored in an individual. Rather, individual mind arises continuously and transiently in relationships between people.[121]

I have witnessed up close in my work how the mood and mindset of a group is influenced by the wider system.

A not uncommon example is a team that is playing reasonably well in its high-profile competition but has lost its last three games. The owner of the club is unhappy with the team's position on the points table and tells the media that. The staff and players see their owner's comments. Social media fixates on this signal. The owner then sends the head coach a terse WhatsApp message relaying how important a win is the following week. The next day the owner speaks with the chief executive demanding an improvement. The chief executive convenes a meeting with the head coach and relays this. The chief executive unsubtly points out in this meeting that the head coach's potential contract extension is in the balance.

The head coach is now in a high state of anxiety. They meet with their staff to plan the week and are noticeably fretful, low in mood and promoting a more conservative game plan. The other coaches mirror this.

When the team trains, the players automatically perceive the fear that has infiltrated the environment. The players particularly notice the changes in body language, tone of voice and the words used and how these deviate from the norm. The players' hormonal states shift. They experience a rising fear of making mistakes – their thinking moves from process to outcome. Because the behaviour of their leaders has suddenly changed, trust levels have lowered.

The team is tight. It loses again and plays poorly, worse than the previous lost matches. Now the team really does have a problem.

This systemic influence on behaviour happens every day in our workplaces and families. The way in which a leader or parent presents themselves can result in individuals marinating in stress hormones with all the performance inhibition that produces. Alternatively, they can engage in a way that has individuals energised and optimistic as they swim in oxytocin, serotonin and dopamine.

None of these influences can be measured to two decimal places. However, the cause and effect are undeniable.

Science is continually deepening our understanding of how these dynamics work.

The starting point is our evolved ability, automatic and mostly unconscious, to scan our environment for potential threats to our safety. This threat detection system underpins much of what we have explored in this book: our need to belong (Chapter 1); our need for a shared identity (Chapter 2); the dynamics of power, cliques and status (Chapter 5) and how trust functions (Chapter 6).

In each of these critical dimensions of social life we are profoundly influenced by micro expressions from others. We are particularly attentive to emotional information.

Within milliseconds we interpret signals from others, toggling through facial expressions, tone of voice, body language, confidence levels, energy levels, physical proximity of people to each other, status signals.

We are motivated and incentivised by smiles, attentive eyes and warm words. We are deterred by sensing negative judgement, anger and withdrawal. We pick up on others' anxiety and our threat detection system tells us there must be something to worry about.

We navigate our lives by these cues.

Sometimes we interpret accurately, other times we are wildly off beam. Then kicks in a bias to synchronise our intentions and emotional state with those around us through mirroring.

In the words of Po Bronson and Ashley Merryman in the excellent *Top Dog*:

Mirror processing is one of the ways people on teams unconsciously influence one another through nonverbal cues . . .

Moods and energy levels are contagious, and you can 'catch'
a sense of urgency from teammates. It's an automatic process,
not something you control.[122]

There is perhaps an overreliance on psychometric and personality profiling tools. Yes, they can provide useful insights, but individuals cannot be analysed in a vacuum. We are profoundly influenced by the people around us at any given moment in time. We do not have one way of being, rather we adapt skilfully to our environment.

From this stream of environmental cues, we swiftly establish what the true standards are within a group. This evidence is infinitely more persuasive than words written on posters, in policies and on whiteboards.

We quickly work out what the real standards are around work ethic, integrity, selflessness, safe challenge, and so on. This is what we mimic.

We read in a policy that bullying is not tolerated, but we see managers intentionally intimidating others. We're told that a work-life balance is important, but we see the norm is to work fourteen-hour days. We have a diversity policy, but those who have status and power come from a homogenous clique. We're informed in our induction to challenge with fresh eyes what we find, but then see that those who do this become excluded. It is related in meetings how creative we are, but we only see conformity around us. We're directed to focus on developing new business, but we are paid according to the time we bill existing clients. We see on a wall that one of our values is humility and then watch our leader publicly claim success after success. We're told on offsites of our rich heritage, then the rest of the year our work is disconnected from any sense of shared purpose or Us story.

We scan real-world evidence. Our unconscious mind sends strong signals first then we cognitively reckon later. It is these cues that represent our tribes' real standards and true identity. This is what will shape our own behaviour.

We can think of these standards as forming a line.

In an inspiring group with strong standards, and lived values, the line is high. Together, we take great pride in living above it. When someone falls below the line it is acknowledged and remedied. We know that living above the line will bring success for the tribe and meaning for individuals. That is where we want to live. We know beautiful things are there.

In teams with poor standards and weak values the line is low. It is a place of existing, not of thriving. We know we are not the best version of ourselves here. Our motivation, confidence and energy are low, like the line. We aspire to belong somewhere else.

James Clear, author of *Atomic Habits*, captures this cause and effect relationship:

> 'I've never seen someone stick to positive habits in a consistent fashion in a negative environment. Maybe you can overpower once or twice, maybe you have the willpower on one day, but if you're constantly fighting against those forces, it's very hard to follow through.'[123]

I've seen world-class performers recruited by struggling organisations with an environment riven by weak standards and a lack of togetherness. The new recruit came from, and flourished in, a group where the line was high. In this new team, the recruit adapts and, largely unconsciously, comes to compromise the standards they arrived with. They underperform relative to expectations. Externally and internally criticism follows and insinuations that the reason for their disappointing performance is a character flaw around greed or not caring. The true cause and effect is missed.

The science around these dynamics in groups should be taught in schools to help us raise healthier families.

Some leaders are onto this, though. They invest time and care in designing and curating an environment that sets the optimal conditions for performance. They target this as a critical area to create competitive advantage.

Time to meet the Seattle Seahawks.

7.4 the longbody

Our ancestors understood that groups share a mood and a mindset. That individuals and the connection between them form a single consciousness. Across the world, cultures have long articulated a spiritual sense of oneness.

Native American Indian nations of the north-east, such as the Iroquois, and of the south-west, such as the Hopi and Navajo, expressed this through an idea known as the 'longbody'.

The longbody looks at a tribe (or team) as a single living organism comprising a network of connections.

These connections go beyond the people immediately around us – they include a sacred connection to ancestors and to the physical place. These connections comprise the tribe's life force and sense of identity. The longbody beautifully mirrors the spiritual framework of my own culture half a world away.

Just as in families, it is the quality of these connections that determine the health of the tribe. This echoes Proteas captain Faf du Plessis' comment after the team renewed its culture in 2016: 'We became healthy again.'

The longbody contemplates that a clique or a single person has the power to shift the collective energy, mood and mindset of the group. One person may come with a warmth and confidence towards others that sends a current of energy into the group.

Selfish and pessimistic attitudes and behaviours lower the group's energy and confidence.

There is a deep awareness that leaders have a disproportionate impact on the environment through the way they present themselves and the words they use.

In this world view, the idea of recruiting 'good people' and then hoping the 'chemistry' works is naive to put it mildly. What is demanded is a constant attention to the connections within a team and an engineering of optimal conditions.

This approach, and the longbody idea itself, influences the team culture of the Seattle Seahawks.

The Seahawks have been one of the best and most consistent teams in the NFL over the past decade under Head Coach Pete Carroll. He sets the scene:

'[It's] something that we refer to as longbody. It's a tribal connection that people get when they operate and they live together and they work together and they eat together, they tell stories together, they hunt together, they play together. It allows for a connection that's energetic that can be so powerful that you can feel the people around you, you can operate in connection with them, you can sense them, feel them, feel their pain, feel their joy. That's what we're trying to do.'[124]

In the most competitive division in the NFL, the Seahawks have made the playoffs in nine of Pete Carroll's eleven seasons in charge, and made back-to-back Super Bowl appearances. They have shown an uncommon ability to overcome significant injuries and disruptions to keep competing and going deep into the playoffs. Tellingly, in the COVID-affected 2020 NFL season, the Seahawks not only won their division again, but were the only one of the thirty-two NFL teams that experienced zero infections. That provides a clue to their extraordinary management, discipline and togetherness.

The Seahawks' genuine connection to the longbody is demonstrated by two moments across those two Super Bowl appearances.

In 2014 the underdog Seahawks won the Super Bowl, beating the Denver Broncos 43–8. After exuberant celebrations on the field and the presentation of the Lombardi Trophy the team retired to the sanctuary of its dressing room under the stadium. There, surrounded by staff and families, Pete Carroll called a final huddle for the team and put his hand high, which the players took a grip of, and said, 'We now have what everyone wants . . .' He was not talking about the trophy, '. . . knowing what it takes to be the very best together.' A heightened sense of oneness.

The following season, the Seahawks again won their conference and made the Super Bowl. This time they lost on the final play of the game to the New England Patriots 28–24 (widely regarded as the greatest NFL team of all time under the leadership of Bill Belichick and Tom Brady). The scenes in the dressing room after this heartbreaking loss could not have contrasted more with the year before. Players were crying, grieving, angry, confused. The team had a long flight back home that evening and met once more the following day. This time Pete Carroll told his team, 'This is going to be painful. We're in this together and we don't heal till everyone heals.' Oneness.

As Michael Gervais told me, 'These were longbody moments.' The focus of the leader was less about outcome and more about the life force and spirit of their team. When these are right, the results take care of themselves.

RELATIONSHIP-DRIVEN

The essence of the longbody is the quality of relationships. This has long been part of Pete Carroll's coaching philosophy:

> 'I really had a desire to see if our way of working with people would work in the NFL. I wanted to see what it would be like if you treated people like they're your very own family, and you care for them that much and you try to help them find their best in every way that you can, not just coach football.'

A visible way in which the value of relationships is demonstrated is how Pete Carroll deals with high-profile mistakes by his players. While his compassion is often noted, what is perhaps missed is the reasoning behind his actions. Michael Gervais described it in this way for me:

> 'It starts with awareness that as a team we value relationships. There comes an aspiration to be great at relationships and understanding that involves being present for others, showing an interest in their wellbeing and displaying care to them.'

An example is the approach to feedback. The focus of feedback is not on single acts, such as high-profile big plays, but always on a 'vision of their potential' that was developed when the player was recruited and is renewed with them each season.

LEARNED OPTIMISM

The Seahawks explicitly anchor their culture in optimism. Michael Gervais more fully defines optimism in this way:

'There is a belief that things are going to work out. Therefore, we can stay in the hard times longer. We know that there will be internal and external struggle on the way.'

Michael sees this definition of optimism as interchangeable with mental toughness ('doing the hard things and sticking to it when the going gets tough').

This focus on driving collective optimism is based on the insight that *homo sapiens* have an inbuilt tendency towards pessimism (defined by Michael as 'this may not work out well, so I'd best hold back or get ready to bail out').

Our bias towards pessimism reflects our survival instinct to avoid threat and pain. In performance, this translates to trying to protect ourselves from disappointment.

Optimism, therefore, has to be learned, as powerfully articulated by researchers such as Martin Seligman. The Seahawks 'teach' optimism through the daily framing and priming that goes into their environment.

To enable this, every moment and every interaction in the environment matters.

The staff and senior players regard themselves as 'walking animations of optimism'.

'Positivity' is not a buzz word at the Seahawks; rather it is seen as a by-product of having an optimistic view of the future.

Crucially, the Seahawks think about optimism not just as a big outcome but the micro choices we make on the way. As Michael puts it: 'These are the waters we swim in.'

PRIME TIME

Michael broke down for me the depth of intent and design thinking in the Seahawks' environment.

First, they start with the science. They identify core insights around human behaviour that they want to drive in the environment. This includes the psychological principles from Abraham Maslow's pyramid of human needs and Albert Bandura's work on self-efficacy as well as self-determination theory.

Each season the staff are reconnected to these principles and coached on how to integrate them into their work and relationships. This is also delivered through a programme for the players of discovery (self-awareness) and mental skills (such as self-talk, visualisation and mindfulness).

Second, the Seahawks developed an identity blueprint that brings these underlying principles to life. This includes an overarching philosophy, themes, standards and their style of play.

Third, every single day, the Seahawks leaders design how to bring this cultural framework to life that day. As Michael Gervais puts it: 'Our philosophy has to line up every day.'

What is often noted by the outside world is the energy, noise and fun in the Seahawks' environment. What is often missed is the detail and spirituality that sits behind it.

The key word here is priming. Every day the environment is intentionally primed to instil energy, optimism and psychological safety. In Michael Gervais' words:

'We want guys to walk into a room and be greeted by others, see smiles and have music playing.'

He says that the presence of these elements acts as an 'inoculation to anxiety'. The priming lowers stress hormones and activates the dopamine, serotonin, oxytocin and endorphin systems.

The *noa* takes the form of fast sharp practices amidst loud music, the incorporation of play and competing into team spaces and plenty of banter. The *tapu* includes a 'no whining' rule, and no swearing or yelling is permitted either. Pete Carroll likens this rich environment to a class in school where a teacher is emanating positivity, laughter and music and you want to be part of it.[125]

This design and engineering approach to culture can be contrasted to many environments where the focus is overwhelmingly on organising tasks.

I've long scratched my head at management guru Peter Drucker's famous line, *Culture eats strategy for breakfast*. For me, culture and strategy must be woven together to make a single basket.

Strategy represents how our purpose has been translated into a vision and then a plan is formed to realise it. However, if the strategy is going to succeed, then the environment has to enable (not disable) the behaviours necessary to deliver it. Culture and strategy need to be on the same page.

I once coached in a financial institution where one of their key strategic buckets was 'innovation', yet in their environment a person needed to go through over ten levels of permissions to get a new sale approved. The environment was silently disabling the strategy.

The Seahawks equally value game planning and curating their environment.

The clarity in which they see their optimal environment and its relentless daily pursuit is uncommon.

While Pete Carroll and Michael Gervais are widely lauded as innovative and even 'new age', they are actually connecting us back to our ancestors' wisdom.

7.5 the flowering

Many of the teachings and insights set out in these pages come together in the acting classes of Ken Rea.

Ken is Professor of Theatre at the Guildhall School of Music and Drama in London and has taught there for forty years. He is a teacher and leader on a mission to unleash talent.

Over the years, Ken has taught students who have gone on to become international stars such as Ewan McGregor, Daniel Craig, Hayley Atwell, Orlando Bloom, Michelle Dockery, Joseph Fiennes, Jodie Whittaker, Paapa Essiedu, Dominic West and Damian Lewis. Ken's journey includes teaching in North America, China, India, Germany, New Zealand and Italy. He's also worked with theatres such as the Royal Shakespeare Company.

Each year, around three thousand aspiring actors audition for twenty-eight places in the school's new intake.

When they arrive at the school the potential for a raging state of nature is high: a diverse group of high-ego, highly talented, ambitious individuals thrown together. For each of them, the Guildhall is potentially a springboard to a glittering career.

Ken is someone I've come to know well and have deep respect for. I see him as someone who our ancestors speak through.

His timeless first task is to create an environment where all can thrive:

'My job is to find commonality within a highly diverse collection of individuals. We select them for their striking individual personalities, but find a way of getting them to work together.'

The first term for the new intake is typically a hotbed of anxiety. The 'laws of the jungle' start to play out from the moment the class gathers.

For the first time, many of the students are surrounded by talent as good as, if not better than, themselves. Many experience 'imposter syndrome' where doubts appear over whether they are good enough to be there; an anxiety that they will be found out at any moment. They have a high sensitivity to how the teaching staff are responding to them and have a particularly acute sensitivity to being judged and excluded.

As with all new groups, they also have a gravitational pull to cliques where there is some form of comfort to be found. All the time, students are manically forming a ladder in their own minds of where they rank and who sits above and below them. Alphas in the group are primed to position themselves as 'top dog'.

Ken has a deep understanding of how the environment he curates will powerfully influence behaviours.

He's developed a method to unleash talent that mirrors the ancient wisdom within this book.

Ken's process of building an optimal environment starts with belonging:

'I assure them that they belong here. I tell them that my job is to bring out their individuality and enhance it, not turn them into clones. I try to convey to them that they have been

289

chosen for their unique personality and we want them to leave with that intact. My job is to enhance their uniqueness through the skills they acquire here.'

Ken explains their three-year journey at Guildhall as a spiral, not a circle. The students do not leave where they started; they leave with the same personality but at a higher level with the skills and experience they acquire.

In the words of my ancestors, the shared experience to come is about enhancing the *mana* of each and every individual.

This is what Ken explains to the class: *There is no template for what you should become – it will be a shared experience of heightening your own uniqueness.*

This sense of belonging is further enhanced by a long-standing ritual at the school where, over an extended period, the students form a circle and are invited to share with their classmates whatever they wish to about themselves.

The second part of Ken's culture build involves connecting the students to a higher purpose than personal ambition – the ancient purpose of theatre and of acting itself.

'I tell them that this is their heritage. It's important to understand their purpose as storytellers. It is beyond entertainment. We talk about the river – that what went before feeds the present and the future. It's our way of talking about our *whakapapa*.'

Ken explains to the students the dual role of actors in the human story. The first role is the 'storyteller' – who strengthens a community by narrating its Us story, including creation myths and oral traditions (such as the *Odyssey* and the *Iliad* from ancient Greece, the Sanskrit epics of *Rāmāyaṇa* and *Mahābhārata* from ancient India and Shakespeare in English).

The second purpose of theatre that Ken articulates is the 'healer' – who brings spiritual healing through their insight and stories.

Ken takes time to explain to students that when an actor's motivation is consumed with ego and desire for personal acclaim, this is sensed by the audience and diminishes their ability to fulfil their higher purpose of storyteller and healer.

Ken then shares with the students the 'Us' story of Guildhall itself. He speaks of the continuity of the culture and environment that they will share with their acclaimed ancestors who took those same classes. This is the *whakapapa* of the school itself.

Ken uses values as shorthand for Guildhall's Us story: 'It is these values that forge our identity' (and connect the students to their illustrious predecessors):

warmth – always working from a generous heart

enthusiasm – an awareness that whatever occurs in the room is infectious, so positivity will energise others but cynicism, fear and meekness will sap energy and trust and vulnerability out of the room (this is the longbody)

generosity – an attitude of seeking to give to others, not taking for one's self

In the foreword to Ken's bestselling book, *The Outstanding Actor*, former student Damian Lewis, star of shows such as *Homeland* and *Billions*, affirms Ken's approach:

There isn't a student that has been taught by Ken Rea that can't do a passable impression of him gesticulating and saying in a nurturing and caring way, 'Yes, yes . . . warmth . . . generosity . . .' – his key words, the words that are central to every bit of teaching he does.

These are the values that anchor classmates to each other and to the shared experience they are about to embark on. The students are given space to translate those values into a mission statement and behavioural code for the year.

This is the ancient way: values, wrapped in stories, that emerge from a shared sense of identity, which are then translated into living standards. This is not a place for whiteboarding new values each year or wallpapering rooms with one-dimensional words.

This work is done before classes commence.

Each of these steps undertaken by Ken creates conditions in which a potential unhealthy state of nature is disrupted. Natural tendencies towards selfishness and harmful rivalry are defused by connecting each person to each other and to something greater than themselves. That is an inherently spiritual exercise.

This deep work is not about creating a 'nice' environment. It is about creating an environment where individuals have the opportunity to fulfil their potential. Ken says:

'We need individuals to achieve mastery within a very close ensemble. We cannot have people disappearing anonymously. We have to have a high trust environment and that is built on belonging and selflessness. All progress happens just outside our comfort zone – their life is to work in that territory.'

Critical in this culture build is promoting vulnerability and risk-taking. This may mean students trying something in front of their peers that may not work. Ken regards the ability to take risks as the hallmark of all great actors. This is the sharp end of psychological safety. Ken believes that it is only possible for everyone to take risks if there is a deep sense of belonging and trust. He understands that he cannot command individuals to be vulnerable and take risks – the environment needs to signal it is safe to do so.

Ken showed me on his bookshelf an actor's manual, *Kadensho*, written six hundred years ago, by the great Japanese Noh actor and playwright Zeami.

Within this book, Ken took me to a passage on the ancient Japanese idea of *hana*, which translates as a sense of 'flowering'. From such places Ken's timeless work is guided.

7.6 bring them home safely

We are often more tender to the dead than to the living
though it is the living who need our tenderness most.
Robert McFarlane in *Underland*

There is something that is often overlooked about the achievements of our ancient Polynesian navigators. Yes, their navigational abilities and voyaging feats were epic. But there was something else that marked navigators such as Kupe out as great leaders – after they achieved their mission, they brought their crew back home safely.

Somewhere in *homo sapien*'s evolutionary story, this fundamental role of the leader – to take care of their people – has lost its sacred place.

Today we see an epidemic of loneliness being suffered, through to an avalanche of allegations of harm in teams across society. The rise of the internet and social media seems to be fuelling an illusion of belonging and a reality of disconnection from real tribes that have always anchored our sense of self. In work, study after study report dysfunction, misalignment and disengagement.

At the heart of this fall is a lack of understanding of how being in families, groups and teams affects our wellbeing.

Our ancestors perhaps better understood than us how our social needs impacted on our emotional and physical health. How our sense of identity is fed by our need to belong; to have a higher purpose; to have shared beliefs; to be part of an Us story.

Beyond these foundations of who we are, our daily experiences in families, teams and groups shape our mood and mindset through the big and small signals they send us and the way the future is framed.

A generation ago my country integrated ancestral wisdom on wellbeing into its public health framework. This wisdom was translated into the concept of a house held up by four interconnected walls: *physical* health, *mental* health, *spiritual* health and *social* health. The foundation of the house is the land – our identity and belonging.

The challenge we all share is to build stronger houses.

RENEWAL

We have crossed this timeless valley together.

As we look back, we see the mist has dissolved now and the sun has broken through. We can see the next generation waiting in the place from which we set off.

As their ancestors, we must remind them that our super strength of forming strong teams must never be taken for granted. That this inheritance more than any other has ensured our ability to compete and survive. But we must be honest and tell them that we lost our way and it is time now for renewal. As our ancestor Sir Māui Pōmare said at the funeral of the prophet Te Whiti in 1907:

'The old order has changed; your ancestors said it would change. When the net is old and worn it is cast aside, the new net goes fishing. I do not want to blame the old net; it was good in its day, and many fish were caught in it. But the old net is worn with time and we must go fishing with the new net our brother has brought us.'

The first step we must take is not hard. We simply have to pause and find a moment of peace. Then, look again at those people we are with and see their *mana*, their spirit, their dignity. Then remind ourselves that whatever we do as a tribe, that must never be diminished.

This is where we can start.

Epilogue

I have spent most of my adult life moving between two places of belonging: New Zealand and England. My wife, Elizabeth, and I have raised our children in both.

Countless times, we have voyaged over those oceans that exacted so much sacrifice and hope from my lines of ancestors.

Over three summers and two winters we lived in a village on the east coast of the North Island of New Zealand. A place close to where Paikea made shore from his epic passage upon the sacred whale. A day's drive from where the *Takitimu* canoe landed with Tahu eight hundred years ago. A bridge away from where my Irish and English ancestors arrived in this country.

It is the place where my Nana Rose, Pakinui's great-grandchild, lived in her old age.

When this was our home, we swam in our small idyllic bay most days of the summer.

Half a mile from this beach is a heart-shaped lake, a volcanic mountain inverted by its final eruption. From this lake freshwater streams run underground to the bay.

These tiny streams come up through the sand and, twisting around black volcanic rocks, run across the beach like the lines of our *whakapapa*. These streams fulfil their destiny in becoming one with the sea. The purity of that stream water remains but its identity is now something else.

It was into these waters of Thorne Bay, over those long summers, that my children emerged baptised with a new sense of their own uniqueness.

In the year that followed, we voyaged back over the oceans to settle in the Cotswolds area of England, close to Elizabeth's family home.

In our first week there, our son Tom joined the Stow-on-the-Wold rugby club's under-elevens' team.

That weekend, the Stow team hosted a rival nearby village. The playing ground perched high on a ridge peering over an endless valley. Snowshill nestled in the distance.

The sidelines were full of people who cared.

At half-time in this tense game the scores were tied.

The rival team gathered at one end of the field. They were a chaotic jumble: some going across to parents, some lying on the ground, some arguing, some nervously awaiting orders. They were apart. Their coach came over barking instructions and substituting players. He pointed to where on the field he wanted his team to play and then bustled off to the sidelines.

Tom's new team was different. No adult went near them. Instead, the coaches stood back and allowed them to manage themselves.

These ten-year-olds put their arms around each other and formed a huddle. The captain spoke a few words. The alphas took their turn. Their heads were high. They looked hard into each other's eyes. There was no distraction or fooling around. Their body language divulged that they were fully in this moment together. In a state of peace with themselves and each other.

Optimism breathed in their circle. A beautifully diverse mix of young people, arms around each other, ascended into a shared mood and mindset that something good was about to happen. They fed on a hormone soup that would allow them to trust each other and access their talent under the scrutiny of those they cared about.

Tom, the youngest in the team, experienced a profound sense of belonging in that huddle despite having met these boys only three days before. In that circle he felt strong.

In creating this communion with each other they had achieved something no scoreboard could document. They had recreated what our ancestors tried so hard to teach us – striving together anchored in a deep sense of belonging.

I watched this from the sidelines. I had not seen this before – young people trusted like that. They had been coached in the days before the game then gifted the freedom to be themselves and create their own destiny. *Tapu* and *noa* were in balance on this day.

As we readied for the second half, we moved closer to the people of this club. They smiled and made a space for us. We joined their line, their *whakapapa*.

In a few moments, the whistle blew, and the game resumed.

In the second half, the Stow team scored four times. Their rivals could not respond. Upon the final whistle, those people who cared about them cheered and the boys celebrated. Then they lined up and shook hands with their rivals.

Elizabeth, Livvy and I moved forward with the line of families and supporters and clapped the boys off the field. Tom, covered in mud, greeted us with the broadest smile, and Livvy went over and hugged him.

As we stood there together on that ancient hill, the sun broke through the clouds for the first time that morning. I watched it gradually move onto my children. They had found a new place of belonging. Another place where they could stand tall.

Notes

1   *Nga Pepeha a nga Tipuna: the sayings of the ancestors,* Hirini Moko
    Mead (2003), Victoria University Press, Wellington, p.9

2   https://www.goodreads.com/quotes/230921-the-cradle-rocks-above-an-
    abyss-and-common-sense-tells

3   'Why Do We See So Many Things as "Us vs. Them"?', David Berreby,
    National Geographic, 12 March 2018, https://www.nationalgeographic.
    com/magazine/2018/04/things-that-divide-us/

4   'Loneliness and social isolation as risk factors for coronary heart disease
    and stroke: a systematic review and meta-analysis of longitudinal obser-
    vational studies', Valtorta N.K., Kanaan M., Gilbody S., et al, Heart
    2016; 102: 1009–1016

5   'Loneliness and Social Isolation as risk factors for mortality: a meta-
    analytic review', Holt-Lunstad J., Smith T.B., Baker M., Harris T.,
    Stephenson D., *Perspectives on Psychological Science,* 2015; 10(2): 227–237

6   'The neural bases of social pain: evidence for shared representations
    with physical pain', Naomi I. Eisenberger, *Psychosomatic Medicine,* 2012
    February; 74(2): 126–135

7   *Behave,* Robert Sapolsky (2017) Penguin Random House USA, pp.112–114

8   'The neural bases of social pain: evidence for shared representations
    with physical pain', Naomi I. Eisenberger, *Psychosomatic Medicine,* 2012
    February; 74(2): 126–135

9   *The Culture Code*, Daniel Coyle (2019) Random House Business, pp.10–11

10 'I just wanted to fit in and feel valued': Bancroft explains his role in ball tampering, *Sydney Morning Herald* (26 December 2018)

11 *Principles of Scientific Management*, F.W. Taylor (1911), New York and London, Harper & Brothers, p.7

12 *Wayfinding Leadership*, Chellie Spiller, Hoturoa Barclay-Kerr & John Panoho, Huia Publishers (2015) pp.64–65

13 Radio New Zealand's Kim Hill interview with Pádraig Ó Tuama, 14 March 2020, https://www.rnz.co.nz/national/programmes/saturday/audio/2018738444/padraig-o-tuama-the-poetry-and-politics-of-kindness

14 'New Zealand are a great rugby team because of their pride in the shirt', Zinzan Brooke (*Daily Telegraph*, 11 September 2015)

15 https://www.youtube.com/watch?v=lewqHaiujsk

16 'A Kaupapa Māori, culturally progressive, narrative review of literature on sport, ethnicity and inclusion', Jeremy Hapeta, Farah Palmer, Yusuke Kuroda & Gary Hermansson (2019), Kōtuitui: New Zealand Journal of Social Sciences Online, 14:2, 209–29, DOI: 10.1080/1177083X.2019.1600558, pp.211–212

17 *Legends in Black: New Zealand Rugby Greats on Why We Win*, Tom Johnson, Penguin Books (2014), p.203

18 *Legends in Black*, Tom Johnson, p.194

19 *Legacy*, James Kerr, Constable (2013), p.133

20 *Legacy*, James Kerr, p.133

21 *Ngai Tahu: a migration history*, Bridget Williams Books, (2008), p.185

22 *The Science of Storytelling*, Will Storr, William Collins (2019), p.155

23 *Us and Them: understanding your tribal mind*, David Berreby, Little Brown & Company (2005), pp.39–40

24 *Us and Them*, David Berreby, p.93

25 *Behave*, Robert Sapolsky, p.388

26 *Behave*, Robert Sapolsky, p.423

27 All in the Mind with Lynne Malcolm podcast (ABC), interview 3 December 2017 with Sarah Gorman

28 All in the Mind with Lynne Malcolm podcast (ABC), interview 3 December 2017 with Sarah Gorman

29 *Behave*, Robert Sapolsky, p.394

30 *The Sea People*, Christina Thompson, William Collins (2019), p.128

31 'The Embers of Society: Firelight Talk among the 69 34 Ju/'hoansi Bushmen', 71 6 Polly Wiessner 74 7 8 University of Utah 270 S. 1400 E. Rm 102 Salt Lake City, Utah, 84112

32 https://hbr.org/2008/02/make-your-good-team-great-1

33 *Senior Leadership Teams: What it Takes to Make Them Great*, Ruth Wageman, Debra A. Nunes, James A. Burruss, J. Richard Hackman, (2008) p.212

34 https://news.gallup.com/businessjournal/195491/few-employees-believe-company-values.aspx

35 'De-Homogenizing American Individualism: Socializing Hard and Soft Individualism in Manhattan and Queens', Adrie Suzanne Kusserow, *Ethos*, vol. 27, no. 2, 1999, pp. 210–234. JSTOR, www.jstor.org/stable/640657. Accessed 9 Feb. 2021

36 *Us and Them*, David Berreby, p.184

37 *The Power Paradox*, Dacher Keltner (2017), Penguin, pp.94–5

38 'Failings of England's "Golden Generation" baffle Man City boss Guardiola', *Goal* (1 April 2017)

39 https://www.theguardian.com/football/2018/jul/03/england-have-created-their-own-history-gareth-southgate-world-cup

40 https://en.wikipedia.org/wiki/Noel_Godfrey_Chavasse

41 'The Role of Ritual in the Evolution of Social Complexity: Five Predictions and a Drum Roll', Harvey Whitehouse, Pieter François, and Peter Turchin (2015), Cliodynamics6: 199–216

42 'The neural bases of social pain: evidence for shared representations with physical pain', Eisenberger NI, *Psychosom Med.* 2012;74(2):126-135

43 *In a League of Their Own*: The Dick, Kerr Ladies, Gail J. Newsham (2018), Paragon Publishing, p.6

44 https://www.quotes.net/mquote/788067, p.10

45 https://www.egonzehnder.com/insight/in-conversation-with-ed-schein

46 *Behave*, Robert Sapolsky, p.273

47 *Behave*, Robert Sapolsky, p.273

48 *Behave*, Robert Sapolsky, p.274

49   *Behave*, Robert Sapolsky, p.274

50   https://scottbarrykaufman.com/what-does-it-mean-to-be-self-actualized-in-the-21st-century/

51   *Sacred Hoops*, Phil Jackson, Hyperion (1995), p.5

52   *I, George Nepia* (2002), London League Publications, pp.107–08

53   *Behave*, Robert Sapolsky, quoting Michigan, Huda Akil, p.70

54   'The rainbow beauty of Hashim Amla', Niren Toisi, *The Cricket Monthly* (4 January 2018)

55   'The rainbow beauty of Hashim Amla', Niren Toisi, *The Cricket Monthly* (4 January 2018)

56   *From Rags to Riches*, Mohammed Al-Fahim (1995), I.B. Tauris, p.185

57   *The Sea People*, Christina Thompson

58   https://www.brainyquote.com/quotes/christopher_columbus_100795

59   https://www.thenational.ae/uae/desert-survival-secrets-of-ancient-bedouin-navigation-1.425342

60   'To Lead, Create a Shared Vision', James M. Kouzes and Barry Posner, *Harvard Business Review* (January 2009)

61   https://www.rochester.edu/pr/Review/V74N4/0402_brainscience.html

62   https://drdavidhamilton.com/real-vs-imaginary-in-the-brain-and-body/

63   https://www.youtube.com/watch?v=CKrgRenPLoY

64   https://www.youtube.com/watch?v=9YgBvKsABV4&t=1937s

65   *Finding Mastery* podcast, Rick Welts interview with Michael Gervais, 24 July 2017, https://findingmastery.net/rick-welts/

66   https://www.youtube.com/watch?v=6qagkaBdOoU

67   https://www.youtube.com/watch?v=FjSpvurd4XM&t=453s

68   *The Cubs' Way*, Tom Verducci (2017), Three Rivers Press, Chapter 5, p. 76

69   *The Cubs' Way*, Tom Verducci, Chapter 6, p.101

70   *Finding Mastery* podcast, Michael Gervais interview with Elizabeth Lindsey (National Geographic explorer), 9 December 2015

71   'Jackie Robinson Breaks Baseball's Color Barrier, 1945' (2005) EyeWitness to History, www.eyewitnesstohistory.com

72   'Branch Rickey Hurls Barbed Insults at Jackie Robinson', Peter Carlson, *American History* (June 2013 issue)

73   https://time.com/4243338/allbirds-wool-runners/

74 *How I Built This* podcast, with Guy Raz, 10 June 2019

75 Rev. James Watkin's journal, 1830–1839, 1840–1882 (MS-0440/004), held in the Hocken Library in Dunedin, New Zealand

76 https://www.brainyquote.com/quotes/sitting_bull_260488

77 *Leviathan*, Thomas Hobbes, chapters XIII–XIV

78 'Can race be erased? Coalitional computation and social categorization', Robert Kurzban, John Tooby and Leda Cosmides, Proceedings of the National Academy of Sciences, 18 December 2001, 98 (26): 15387–15392

79 *Behave*, Robert Sapolsky, p.475

80 *Behave*, Robert Sapolsky, p.88

81 'The process of status evolution', Fisek, M.H. and Ofshe, R. (1970), *Sociometry*, 33, 327–346 in *Evolutionary Psychology*, David Buss (5th edition), pp.348–49

82 'Hierarchisation and dominance assessment at first glance', Kalma, A. (1991), *European Journal of Social Psychology*, 21, 165–181 in *Evolutionary Psychology*, Buss (5th edition), p.349

83 'Social norms and other minds: the evolutionary roots of higher cognition', D.D. Cummins and C. Allen (Eds), *The Evolution of Mind* (1998), Oxford University Press, pp.30–50, in *Evolutionary Psychology*, Buss (5th edition), p.361

84 *Evolutionary Psychology*, David Buss (5th edition), p.372

85 *Behave*, Robert Sapolsky, p.132

86 *Us and Them*, David Berreby, p.263

87 *The Power Paradox*, Dacher Keltner, p.68

88 *The Power Paradox*, Dacher Keltner, p.56

89 *Evolutionary Psychology*, David Buss (5th edition), p.369

90 'The pursuit of status in social groups', Anderson, C. & Kilduff, G.J. (2009), *Current Directions in Psychological Science*, 18, 289–295 in *Evolutionary Psychology*, Buss (5th edition), p.352

91 *Sacred Hoops*, Phil Jackson, p.6

92 *Sacred Hoops*, Phil Jackson, p.109

93 *Us and Them*, David Berreby, p.275

94 *Evolutionary Psychology*, David Buss (5th edition), pp.358–360

95 *The Power Paradox*, Dacher Keltner, p.43

96 *The Power Paradox*, Dacher Keltner, p.43

97 'Eating Christmas in the Kalahari', Richard Borshay Lee, *The Journal of American Museum of Natural History*, Vol. LXXVIII no.10 (December 1969)

98 '144 Years After the Battle of Little Bighorn, Lakota Values Endure', Mandy Van Heuvelen, *Smithsonian Magazine* www.smithsonianmag.com (24 June 2020)

99 *Good to Great*, Jim Collins (2001), Random House Business, p.20

100 *Good to Great*, Jim Collins, p.27

101 *Good to Great*, Jim Collins, p.27

102 'South Africans pin hopes on rugby win to lift gloom of troubled country', Jason Burke, *Guardian* (1 November 2019)

103 *The Nurture Assumption: Why Children Turn Out the Way They Do*, Judith Rich Harris, The Free Press (1998)

104 'Gareth Southgate: I carried Euro '96 with me for more than 20 years', Paul Henderson, *GQ Magazine* (6 May 2020)

105 Coates, J. M. & Herbert, J. Proc. Natl Acad. Sci. USA 104, 6167–6172 (2008)

106 'Unconscious Discrimination of Social Cues from Eye Whites in Infants', Sarah Jessen, Tobias Grossmann, Proceedings of the National Academy of Sciences USA, 11 November 2014; 111(45): 16208–13

107 'Why Seahawks coach Pete Carroll's compassionate leadership approach could be more important than ever', Larry Stone, *Seattle Times* (30 June 2020)

108 'Gareth Southgate: I carried Euro '96 with me for more than 20 years', Paul Henderson, *GQ Magazine* (6 May 2020)

109 '"I really feel part of the English tradition" says Billy Vunipola', Mick Cleary, *Daily Telegraph* (27 October 2013)

110 'Managing Relationship Decay Network, Gender, and Contextual Effects', Sam B.G. Roberts and R. I. M. Dunbar, *Human Nature* (2015), 26: 426–450

111 *Drive*, Daniel Pink, Riverhead Books (2009), p.71 & p.108

112 'Sergei Polunin: ballet's bad boy opens up about love, dance and rebellion', Ella Alexander, *Harper's Bazaar* (13 March 2017)

113 *The Dancer* (2016) directed by Steven Cantor

114 https://www.ted.com/talks/brene_brown_the_power_of_vulnerability?
    language=en#t-24406

115 *Behave*, Robert Sapolsky, pp.458–59

116 *Behave*, Robert Sapolsky, p.477

117 *Hagakure*, Yamamoto Tsunetomo, (2014 edition), p.50

118 *Finding Mastery* podcast interview with Shaka Smart (16 August 2017)

119 *The Troopers' Tale*, Don McKay Turnbull Ross Publishing (2012),
    pp.186–195

120 *New Zealand in the First World War 1914–1918: New Zealand Artillery
    in the Field 1914–18*, Lieutenant J. R. Byrne (Whitcombe and Tombs Ltd,
    1922), p.135

121 *Complex Responsive Processes in Organisations*, R.D. Stacey (2001),
    Routledge, New York, p.5

122 *Top Dog*, Po Bronson and Ashley Merryman (2014), Ebury Press, p.196

123 https://www.youtube.com/watch?v=U_nzqnXWvSo

124 Finding Mastery podcast interview of Pete Carroll by Michael Gervais (9
    October 2019)

125 Finding Mastery podcast interview of Pete Carroll by Michael Gervais (9
    October 2019)

Acknowledgements

For their direction and encouragement, Rory Scarfe, Neil Blair, Richard Milner and the teams at Quercus and Hachette.

With deep thanks to the generous people who shared their stories and wisdom in these pages, just as their ancestors had with them.